Our Santiniketan

THE INDIA LIST

MAHASWETA DEVI

Our Santiniketan

Translated by Radha Chakravarty

LONDON NEW YORK CALCUTTA

Seagull Books, 2022

Originally published in Bengali as *Amader Santiniketan*
© Tathagata Bhattacharya

First published in English translation by Seagull Books, 2022
English translation © Radha Chakravarty, 2022

ISBN 978 0 8574 2 901 8

British Library Cataloguing-in-Publication Data
A catalogue record for this book is available from the British Library

Typeset by Seagull Books, Calcutta, India
Printed and bound the USA by Integrated Books International

Contents

The Past Is a Place:
Mahasweta Devi and the Memory of Santiniketan
RADHA CHAKRAVARTY

> Like a dazzling feather that has fluttered down from some unknown place. In my mind it remains, enclosed within a box made of glass. I can turn it this way and that, look at it from any angle, whenever I desire [. . .] How long will the feather keep its colours, waiting? The 'feather' stands for memories of childhood. Memories don't wait [. . .]

Amader Santiniketan, here translated as *Our Santiniketan*, was first published in Bengali by Srishti Prakashan in 2001, on the occasion of Boimela, the annual Book Fair in Kolkata. Vividly narrated in the voice of the ageing Mahasweta Devi as she struggles to recapture vignettes of her childhood days in Santiniketan as a schoolgirl in the 1930s, these reminiscences bring to the written page her individual sensibility and the ethos of a remembered place in a remembered time. Seen through the innocent eyes of a young girl, a forgotten Santiniketan comes to life—the place, its people, flora and fauna, educational environment, culture of free creative expression, vision of harmonious coexistence between natural and human worlds, and above all, the towering presence of Tagore himself. Alongside, we get a glimpse of the private Mahasweta—her inner life, family and associates, and the early experiences that shaped her personality.

Despite pressure from readers, scholars and publishers, Mahasweta never wrote a full-fledged autobiography, although she expressed a desire to do so. Between 1977 and 2014, she published numerous scattered writings on her life and times, unfinished fragments that nevertheless offer a window to the inner and outer worlds she inhabited during her long, chequered career. Perhaps the most sustained attempt at autobiographical writing can be found in the short pieces serialized in the journal Proma between 1996 and 2002, with the title *Ek Jibonei*. But the series remains incomplete, breaking off abruptly, with an unpublished handwritten fragment discovered after her death, and later added to the updated version of the series included in *Ek Jibonei: Smritikatha Sangraha* (2017), a compendium of Mahasweta's life writings. While writing these pieces for *Proma*, Mahasweta wrestled with her failing health and fading memory. As Ajoy Gupta, editor of *Ek Jibonei*, points out in his Preface to the volume, she left it too late, and her long-awaited memoirs remained incomplete in more senses than one.

Meanwhile, *Amader Santiniketan* appeared in 2001. At several points, the narrative mentions, yet refuses to name, the person who persuaded Mahasweta to take up this project. That unnamed person was Alok Chattopadhyay, then editor of Srishti Prakashan, the publishing house that brought out the book. In this brief but intense memoir, Mahasweta reminisces about her early schooldays, from 1936 to 1938, the years she spent at Santiniketan, amidst the natural surroundings of Birbhum in West Bengal, in the living presence of Rabindranath Tagore. The title of her book echoes the opening words of the Santiniketan anthem, a Tagore lyric asserting a passionate sense of belonging to the place:

amader Santiniketan
amader shob hotey apon

Our very own Santiniketan
Dearest to our hearts

Mahasweta's reminiscences capture the spirit of the song, conjuring up a glowing image of Santiniketan as an idyllic haven in a bygone era, a place that left a permanent imprint on the hearts of those who came to know it closely. The book is dedicated to Bappa—her son Nabarun Bhattacharya—estranged from her since she left his father, her first husband, Bijan Bhattacharya. 'I gift you the most carefree days of my own childhood,' she writes. 'Let my childhood remain in your keeping.'

The text enacts Mahasweta's attempts to traverse the difficult terrain of memory, as she encounters her own bouts of amnesia as well as the temporal and geographical distance that separates the Santiniketan of the 1930s from Kolkata at the end of the millennium. The narrative recaptures, retrospectively, the young Mahasweta's pre-school days, her rage, shock and bitterness against her family for sending her away to boarding school, her arrival at Santiniketan, followed by her first impressions, initiation into, and ultimate integration with, the mode of education and way of life that made the place a world unto itself.

Our Santiniketan testifies to the formative and lasting influence of Tagore and his visionary educational experiment on Mahasweta Devi, although her own trajectory as a firebrand writer-activist appears so markedly different from Tagore's. 'Discerning people can see the influence,' Mahasweta insists. 'From Santiniketan I have received the inspiration to work tirelessly and continuously. [. . .] The influence is there, I feel; it requires analysis.'[1] Everywhere in *Our Santiniketan*, we feel the

---

1 Anindya Sourabh, 'Mahasweta Debir Mukhomukhi' [Bengali]. Interview with Mahasweta Devi on 28 December 2003, at the author's

presence of Tagore. 'To me, "Santiniketan" is synonymous with Rabindranath,' she declares, and adds: 'I feel that whatever my writings have to offer (if anything), about forests, adivasis, rural people—he is at the source of it all.'[2] In brief, witty anecdotes, she describes Tagore's way with children, and the informal interactions she and her companions enjoyed with him as a child. 'I had complained to Rabindranath: "Don't write so much, I can't read all that stuff," she recounts wryly, in an interview. 'Those were our childhood days, after all.'[3]

Through lively vignettes of her student life in Santiniketan during the 1930s, she offers us glimpses of Tagore's innovative ideas on education as they were implemented in practice. '[T]hey would plant in our minds the seeds of great philosophical ideals, like trees,' muses Mahasweta. ' "Education" means building physical fitness [. . .] And in order to mould human character, to train people to be active, efficient, free-spirited and confident, you must plant the seeds in early childhood itself. [. . .] Open their mind's eye. Let their inner eye learn to observe'.[4] Children were encouraged to approach learning with an open, curious mind, and to absorb life-lessons through direct interactions with their surroundings. The methods, Mahasweta's text demonstrates, were unorthodox: 'A work schedule, indeed! Identifying trees,

---

Golf Green residence, printed in *Amritalok* (2005). Reprinted in *Aksharekha* 11(1) (September 2018; special issue on Mahasweta Devi, edited by Nilkamal Sarkar): 62. [All the Bengali citations herein are in my translation.—Trans.]

2 Mahasweta Devi, *Ek Jibonei: Smritikatha Sangraha* [Bengali]. (Ajoy Gupta ed.) (Kolkata: Dey's Publishing, 2017), p. 404, p. 422.

3 Amar Mitra, 'Mahaswetadir Mukhomukhi' [Bengali]. Interview with Mahasweta Devi. *Pustakmela* (January–March 2010). Reprinted in *Aksharekha* (2018): 37.

4 *Our Santiniketan*, p. 32.

raiding fruit trees, and in the rains, running towards the Kopai with Jiban-da and Sudhir Gupta-da, all of us getting soaked together, learning how to swim as we plunged about in those red, muddy waters during that downpour'.[5]

The reminiscences also reveal a shared interest in nature, environment and ecology that connects Tagore's vision of coexistence between human, natural and animal worlds to Mahasweta's later environmental activism. Nature is as much a living presence in the young Mahasweta's consciousness as the human community at Santiniketan. 'We were taught in our school at Santiniketan that every animal, every cat, every bird, had a right to live,' she declares. 'From childhood, we were taught to care for nature, not to break a single leaf or flower from a tree. Today, when the planet Earth is endangered, Tagore's teachings are doubly relevant.'[6] She speaks eloquently of the formative influence of Santiniketan on her worldview and work ethic: 'Forests, trees, creatures of the wilds, at the root of my profound love for all these lies the Santiniketan of my childhood. And the training to continue one's work in the face of a hundred obstacles—that, too, has its roots in Santiniketan.'[7] Santiniketan's special gift to her, she claims, is the awakening of her social conscience: 'Had I not lived in Santiniketan during those times, my ear would not have become attuned to hearing the unspoken utterances of mute humanity. [. . .] I would not have been moulded into the kind of person I am.'[8]

---

5 *Our Santiniketan*, p. 47.
6 Mahasweta Devi, 'Introduction' in Rabindranath Tagore, *The Land of Cards: Stories, Poems and Plays for Children* (Radha Chakravarty trans.) (New Delhi: Penguin, 2010), p. *viii*.
7 *Ek Jibonei*, p. 422.
8 *Ek Jibonei*, p. 422.

In these pages, we encounter a host of personages: Rabindranath's children Rathindranath and Mira, his daughter-in-law Pratima Devi, and many others in the Tagore circle, including Nandalal Bose, Ramkinkar Baij, Rani Chanda, Amiya Chakravarty and Tejeschandra Sen. Alongside these luminaries, the workers of Santiniketan also come vividly to life: Kalo and his shop, Bhola, Hari and Prabhakar, the 'kitchen army', Sudha-di, Nalini-di and Harani-didi the women caregivers at the girls' hostel, and Jaidev, the man with the burn-scar on his face: 'Jaidev squatting in his deserted shop, kettle on the boil. In front of him, a sleeping dog, its tail curled up. I found this image as soon as I searched for it. There's a picture gallery in my mind'.[9] The intimacy of a small community is evoked through anecdotes about the hostel and kitchen staff, teacher-student relationships, and escapades with friends and fellow students. In the 2003 interview with Anindya Sourabh, Mahasweta insists that those days of a close-knit community, and the sense of belonging that Santiniketan inspired, are gone: 'The Santiniketan that you all know is not the place it used to be. Our Santiniketan was a small place.'[10]

Our Santiniketan also bears witness to cultural history in the making. In one memorable episode, the entire Santiniketan community gathers to listen to the first gramophone recording of a song performed by Mohor, the young singing prodigy (later renowned as the Rabindrasangit exponent Kanika Bandyopadhyay). The text captures the magic of that remembered moment through the child Mahasweta's wide-eyed wonder at this new marvel, but in narrating a collective experience, it also reflects the innocence and simplicity of an entire society at the threshold of a technological revolution.

9 *Our Santiniketan*, p. 21.
10 Sourabh, 'Mahasweta Debir Mukhomukhi', p. 62.

Nostalgia for the simple dignity of a bygone era colours the entire narrative. Such nostalgia goes hand in hand with implicit social critique and reflections on the present. Mahasweta bemoans, for instance, the failure of modern India to live up to Tagore's ideals. 'Rabindranath's major legacy lies in his thoughts on child education. Rabindranath transformed these ideas into reality [. . .] Yet, fifty-nine years after Independence, Bengalis have not understood the meaning of the word "education", even now.'[11]

Our Santiniketan simultaneously captures the immediacy of the child's eye perspective while offering a window to the adult author's mature worldview. A critique of colonialism emerges in the early chapters, through the evocation of remembered details, such as the description of train compartments in the 1930s, when the white sahebs travelled First Class while Indians were assigned separate compartments or Second and Third Class berths. The architecture and décor in Santiniketan, defined by simple elegance and indigenous materials, and cited as a marker of Tagore's contribution to the development of Bengali taste, are contrasted with the ostentation of official bungalows constructed and furnished in the colonial style. The author's childhood experiences are mediated by the political and historical awareness of her later, more mature self.

More important than all the details that crowd this little book, however, are the gaps, silences and uncertainties that form an intrinsic part of its texture. When writing *Our Santiniketan*, Mahasweta was wrestling with a failing memory. She was sometimes unwilling to acknowledge this. In an interview with Joya Mitra, Mahasweta denies that her memory can prove treacherous, laying claim to the authenticity of her own life-narrative:

---

11 *Our Santiniketan*, p. 32.

'No one can remember as much as I do, about my own life. [. . .] My life is my own.'[12] Yet, with disarming frankness, the text often falters in its recapitulation of factual details, and leaves many questions unanswered. At one point, she pauses to wonder: 'Diving into the ocean of memory and retrieving one water-soaked photograph after another, am I recounting all the details accurately?'[13] Such moments of self-doubt signal the lapses in memory that haunted her in the last years of her life. They also create the image of an unreliable narrator, not always sure of her facts. To an extent, all memoirs, despite their ostensible truth claims, can be considered 'unreliable', because they contain reminiscences filtered through the author's subjectivity. In Mahasweta's reminiscences, though, the narrative sometimes openly abandons its claims to accuracy, acknowledging frequent failures of memory

With its patchwork effect, selective use of facts and its fragmentary, whimsical mode of narration punctuated with digressions and asides, the text cannot be labelled an autobiography in the traditional sense. As Sudhir Chakrabarti says: 'Mahasweta is aware that she is not the kind of person to accept the prevalent colonial definition of autobiography. [. . .] As a creative writer of fiction and a talented writer of prose, she has in her own way invented a new narrative model, adding ingredients of affect and colour to her mode of expression.'[14] In this unorthodox model, we discover a fascinating if disconcerting mix of fact and myth-making, sharp recall and bewildered forgetting, fragments of an

---

12 Joya Mitra, 'Mukhomukhi' [Bengali]. Interview with Mahasweta Devi, *Aksharekha* (2018): 85.
13 *Our Santiniketan,* p. 58.
14 Sudhir Chakrabarti, 'Ek Jibaner Ashesh Gatha' [Bengali], *Aksharekha* (2018): 96.

individual life interwoven with multiple others, and a rooted, localized narrative that expresses broad, universal concerns. Mahasweta's text draws us in with what it tells, yet baffles us with what it withholds or reinvents, teasing us with its silences, uncertainties and incompleteness. Vividly present to our imagination, yet beyond the reach of our lived reality, a remembered Santiniketan hovers in the pages of the book, just like the dazzling but elusive feather inside locked up treasure box of Mahasweta's memory.

Bappa,

Both of us lost our childhood at the age of thirteen.

Now, turning my back on the west, I am walking backwards,

towards your childhood. On the way, I gift you the most

carefree days of my own childhood.

Let my childhood remain with you.

Ma

31 January 2001

First Sight

I first visited Santiniketan at the age of four, I'm told.

If we calculate the date, that would be 1930, or December 1929. Whether it was that December, or the January of 1929, I don't know. Ma said it was an awfully cold winter. Shivering all the way on our journey there, shivering all the way back.

How amazing! I used to remember my very, very young days very, very well.

Yet now I can no longer recall that first visit.

I can't be expected to remember, either. For now, I'm in my seventy-fifth year.

For a long, long time, I lived with Ma, Baba, my mamas, mashis, kakas, pishis, Dadu, Didima, Thakurda (only I called him 'Dada'), Thakuma—all of them.

Not just them. Also Ma's kaka, jyatha, mama, mashi, and their children and grandchildren. In other words, I lived with relatives of a hundred kinds, our lives closely entangled. For as long as they were with us, there was constant talk. In that buzz of conversation, one heard people say things like:

'You were four years old then!'

'When you fell off the tree . . . '

'The time you boarded an aeroplane . . . '

That was how one got to know about one's own childhood. So many years since Ma left us—to whom can I narrate my tales of childhood now! What I want to say here is that, although my first visit to Santiniketan was something that really happened, it's an event I know of only by hearsay.

What we learn of by hearsay can also be true, after all. Way back in 1936, I went to Jhargram. Those days, Jhargram was a sea of sal forests.

Like an island within that sea was a house where we stayed. When Baba was transferred to Medinipur, I got to see a great deal of the Gopa, Jhargram, Salbani, Belpahari of those times.

'Khuku! In Medinipur we spent our happiest days,' Ma used to say.

I say the same.

Look, I'll tell you about my childhood. But there's no one alive now who can understand what I'm talking about.

Never mind. I must talk about the first time I saw Santiniketan.

Baba had probably joined Visva-Bharati as a member. What was his reason?

Visva-Bharati was Rabindranath's creation, after all!

Well, Baba had seen Rabindranath several times, gone to meet him as well. This time, he had decided to take Ma with him, and us two sisters too.

If I was four at the time, my sister Mitul would have been no more than six months old!

Trains those days had First Class, Second Class, Inter Class and Third Class compartments. We boarded a Second Class compartment. A pair of wide, leather-upholstered berths below, another pair above.

In addition, the First Class compartment had a wall-mounted mirror, and hooks to hang clothes, raincoats and umbrellas. Fixed to the wall between the two bathrooms was a table with no legs. As far as I can remember, these items were absent from the Second Class compartment. The cushioning of the First Class berths was heavier, and the other fittings much superior. White sahebs and brown sahebs, did they all travel First Class? I don't know.

That they didn't travel in the same compartment, was something I heard of all the time. The British were in power then. They were the ruling class.

Gandhiji always travelled Third Class, in compartments meant for common people. Incredible, as it seems today, once I saw Gandhiji too; but let that be.

Anyway, it was high winter then. On the train, Ma and I took the lower berth. A gentleman on the berth above us, another on the lower berth opposite. Baba on the upper berth, with Mitul. Ma and Baba had a massive war of words, I'm told.

'You take the upper berth with Khuku. Mitul is so tiny, let her remain with me.'

'Aha! You can recline comfortably.'

'Mitul is so small, she'll fall off!'

'How can she, when I'm with her?'

And so, the verbal battle went on and on. The gentleman on the lower berth interrupted from time to time, saying things like:

'Aha! Please stop this! The children are asleep after all, so why must you . . . ?' and so on.

Ultimately, at some point, everyone fell asleep. Look, among all the trains of those days—BNR, INR, this Mail, that Mail, some other Mail—which one we were travelling in, I can't say. I'm told that the moment we arrived at Bhedia station, it was either our co-passengers who declared: 'This is Bolpur', or my Baba who decided, 'This is Bolpur'. How exactly it happened, there's no way of figuring out now, after a gap of seventy years. From what I knew of my Baba, I suspect he tumbled out of the train, announcing:

'This is Bolpur!'

Ma recounted how, as soon as he alighted at the station, Baba cried, 'We've got off at Bolpur, so why is this station named Bhedia?'

'Bhedia' was the name displayed at the station, on a square glass chimney atop a heavy wooden stand.

Anyway. The station master emerged. He understood the situation and organized a bullock cart for us. It was lined with a thick layer of straw, covered by a shataranchi. You wouldn't know this, but if you sleep on a thick layer of straw with that chequered rug spread over it, it really keeps the cold at bay. Dumka in 1944, Ghatsila in 1945, I remember them very well. In December, we had travelled to those places from Santi-niketan.

In that bitter cold, my parents had climbed on to the bullock cart and eventually arrived at Santiniketan. The house behind the Mandir, which I thought of as the Guest House since 1936, is where I think they had stayed.

In the morning, they set out for an audience with the poet. Seated beside Rabindranath was Ramananda Chattopadhyay. I was terribly precocious, and even more artless. Apparently, I asked Ramananda Chattopadhyay:

'Are you Robi Thakur?'

Tell me, how was I to blame! Dadu-Didima, my grand-parents back home, used the name 'Robi Thakur'. Thakurda, my paternal grandfather, would say 'Robi-babu'. I mean, he referred to the Poet as 'Robi-babu'. Baba, Boromama, Ma, my mashis and pishis—they used the name 'Rabindranath'. No wonder I had blurted out such a foolish question.

Even that anecdote is a matter of hearsay, after all.

What happened after this episode, I can't recall.

So those were my first glimpses of Rabindranath, and of Santi-niketan.

The Santiniketan I saw six years later, when I went there at the age of ten—that is what remains etched in my memory as 'our Santiniketan'. Like a dazzling feather that has fluttered down from some unknown place. In my mind it remains, enclosed within a box made of glass. I can turn it this way and that, look at it from any angle, whenever I desire.

I can. It's something I can do, even now. Still, I have travelled a long distance away from my childhood, so the glass box now seems far, far away. I gaze at it and realize that the colours are fading. I realize that, one day, all the colours will vanish.

Of course, they will vanish. Someday, someone will ask me to write about it, and with my dimming vision I will sit down to write. Sixty-four years now. How long will the feather keep its colours, waiting?

The 'feather' stands for memories of childhood.

Memories don't wait either. Memories grow tired. They want to go to sleep.

Next

If I don't say a little about the beginnings of my reading and education, it won't be clear why I went to Santiniketan.

My education began when I was very tiny, I'm told. 'Began' is not the right word. It would be correct to say that I made a beginning.

That period in my life goes back to the late 1930s.

Baba was in Jalpaiguri then. Since he had a government job, he had to move from place to place. Baba would get transferred frequently too. Here today, someplace else tomorrow. Jalpaiguri, Mymensingh, Faridpur, Dinajpur, Dhaka—between 1930 and 1935, we were constantly on the move.

I remember that house in Jalpaiguri very well. Our little house was brightly painted. Those days, the government quarters for personnel on transfer used to be whitewashed, the doors and windows painted green. Sometimes they would paint the outside yellow. In front of our house in Jalpaiguri was a vast field. And beyond that, the Teesta river.

During our stay at that house, a series of exciting things happened.

One day, Ma discovered that I had become acquainted with the alphabet. She saw me trying to read the Bengali newspaper. That was enough to make her realize that her occasional attempts to place the primers *Barnaparichay* and *Sahaj Path* in my hands had borne fruit.

I could recognize letters of the alphabet, was reading words, loved reading.

After that incident, what book my studies started with I can't remember. But as far back as my memory takes me, I think I was always looking for a chance to pick up a book and hide somewhere, to read in secret. And from what Ma and others have told me, I was addicted to reading from my youngest days.

Tutul (I called Baba 'Tutul') was delighted. Still so tiny and she's learnt to read! No more worries. Keep buying her books.

I don't know since when I have been reading books, but it seems like forever. As for my Baba, Ma, kaka, pishi, mama, mashi—they were bookworms, all of them. Didima, Thakuma, even they were always with books in their hands.

Didima's collection of Bengali books was incredible. Like other book addicts, I too started reading adult books as a child.

Nobody thought of sending us to school. Reportedly, in my infancy I had once joined Eden Montessori School. Ferrying me to school, somewhere along the way, Mejomama, my mother's second brother Debu Chaudhuri, fell off Baba's motorcycle along with me. That scar under his eyebrow, is it still there or has it gone? So that was the end of my Montessori education.

In 1935, when Baba was in Medinipur, I was admitted to Class Four at the Mission School. 'Put her in school, put her in school,' Ma would keep urging. Baba would listen to her in silence. Then suddenly I was admitted to Class Four, and Mitul to Kindergarten or some other class.

Before that, Mitul used to play with three dictionaries at home, put them to sleep, caress them, and so on. She'd never had any schooling until then. And I was happily riding bicycles, reading books and playing with friends. I was the one who went to school. A tutor used to come home, to try to teach Mitul and Anish.

It was during my days at the Mission School that my third sister was born. We were in Dhaka then.

Everyone scolded Tutul severely, accusing him of being indifferent about our education. They said many other things in the same vein.

Those days Chhotomama, my mother's youngest brother Sankho Chaudhuri, lived in Santiniketan. He had gone there to study for his Bachelor's degree. After graduation, he joined Kala Bhavana.

Why I was sent to Santiniketan was something I often wondered about, later on. Tutul had many connections there, of course. And Ma's maternal cousin Amiya Chakravarty was the Poet's secretary, at one time. Chhotomama was there as well. In one voice, everyone (from Ma's side of the family) declared that a person with a transferable job must place his children somewhere so they could receive an education.

That 'somewhere' was Santiniketan. That the Santiniketan of those few years I spent there would come to occupy the place 'closest to my heart' in my memory, was something I didn't realize at the age of ten.

Right from those times, I was very partial to my mother. When I heard that I would have to leave her and go away, I became tearful. When Ma went over to Baba's side, I felt unbearably bitter and reproachful.

The house from where I departed for Santiniketan was my maternal grandfather's property in Dhaka, at 15 Zindabahar Lane, Armanitola. I left in 1936. Now I write this in December 2000. In sixty-four years, not only Dhaka-Kolkata-Faridpur-Rangpur but even the Bahrampur I first saw in 1945 has really, really changed.

But the old cities live on in secret, hiding here and there. That is something to rejoice about, a matter of great solace. When I went to Dhaka, I didn't search for Tikatuli, Kayettuli, the field at Ramna, Picture Palace at Armanitola—all those places so glowingly etched in my memory. I was terribly afraid that I wouldn't recognize anything, that everything had been utterly transformed. But Rashid Haider assured me:

'Didi! Your grandfather's house remains exactly as it was.'

This proved to be a dazzling reality.

Somehow, the house has survived. Why has it survived? Because the house is now a police outpost. A full-fledged police station is a phanri, what they call a thana. Some thanas have a younger brother. That younger brother is known as the phanri, or outpost.

What a priceless gift the city of Dhaka had given me! When I beheld the house, that was how I felt. It was like finding that proverbial single jewel, the fabled treasure of seven kings. Readers, if you happen to be youngsters of seventy or sixty or fifty, then you will have listened to or read fairy tales in your childhood. You know, of course, how the princes in fairy tales performed such daring feats to gain possession of the seven kings' treasure, that single jewel. That unique jewel, the seven kings' treasure, signifies a possession that is priceless. Say, for instance, I chance upon a letter from my mother! That, too, would be an invaluable possession!

And the house where I was born, where I lived for so long, every nook and cranny etched in my memory—seeing that house still standing, exactly the same after sixty years, I was beside myself with joy.

'O house!' I exclaimed inwardly. 'After 1936 I never came back. And in 1996, there you are, just as before!'

On the terrace of that very house I had wept because I had to leave for Santiniketan to take up my studies. Even at the age of ten, I was told again and again: You're a big girl now, a big girl now. When you become a big girl, you can't cry in front of the others!

Let me tell you about the preparations for my departure. The rules and regulations of Visva-Bharati, published in 1923, arrived by post. Baba read aloud from it:

'A steel trunk . . . '

'A bucket . . . '

'A set of dishes: plate, bowl and glass . . . '

'Gamchha . . . '

'Red-bordered sari . . . '

'Black-bordered sari . . . '

Probably the list also included bed linen, a mosquito net and other such items.

'But Khuku (that was my pet name) doesn't wear saris!' Ma protested.

'She will! Wait and see! Sending our daughter so far away to study. That's your decision, not mine!'

Pretending to be asleep, I was listening to everything they said. Tutul was pacing up and down inside the room.

'She's still so young. All the time I hear it said that she's a big girl now! Anyway, do as you please. What do I care! I'll go, drop her there and come right back.'

'Won't you stay on for a couple of days?'

'And will you take on my office duties during that time?'

Those saris and all the other stuff must have been provided. That trunk was massive.

You'll roll over laughing hearing this, but the frocks and other garments we wore were all homemade. That clothes for infants and children could be purchased or tailored was something nobody was aware of at that time. Not only us, nobody else knew either. Today, who will believe me if I tell them that in 1947, before my wedding, I sewed my own blouses and other garments at home? So, before I left for Santiniketan, Chhoto-mashi and Ma sewed several frocks for me. What other preparations they made, I can't remember.

Angry and upset, I boarded the steamer from Narayanganj, along with Tutul. The Dhaka Mail train from Sealdah to Goalanda, then the steamer to Narayanganj, and after that, the train to Dhaka—that was the route one had to take, those days.

On the steamer, as we sat down to dinner, Tutul patted my back. It was his way of expressing sympathy.

'Eat properly,' he coaxed me.

I wept as I swallowed the chicken stew. Those days, if one ordered chicken stew, curry, roast or korma upon boarding the steamer, they would prepare the dish of one's choice. If one travelled in the daytime, for instance, they would serve us seasonal hilsa curry or some other such item. Now, this sounds like the stuff of ancient lore.

When we alighted in Kolkata, Tutul examined the contents of the trunk.

It was high winter, in the month of December.

Tutul took me to a store in Chowringhee that sold foreign goods. He bought me warm skirts, frocks and so on (thank goodness he got those things for me!), hair oil, soap, cold cream and sundry such items. And he bought me Bata shoes.

It is worth mentioning that we used to get off the train in shoes, and put them back on when returning home. Santiniketan followed a tradition of going barefoot, but I didn't know that then.

At night we again boarded the Second Class compartment of a train. Then Tutul suddenly remembered that I had once asked for ice-cream. The Howrah Station of those days was incredible. Tutul brought me four ice-creams at one go. Those days, 'ice-cream' meant the brand 'Happy Boy'. In the streets of Kolkata roamed their cycle vans, a deep shade of orange. On one side was painted a one-anna coin, in deep blue. On the other side were emblazoned the words: 'Stop Me, and Buy One'.

It is necessary to explain the term 'one anna'.

Those days, the mathematics of coins went like this:

Three pais = one paisa

Twelve pais = one anna or four paisa

Sixteen annas = one rupee.

And one paisa meant two adhuli. Sixteen paisas to one siki. Two sikis to one adhuli. Two adhulis or four sikis to one rupee. But sixty-four paisas also made one rupee.

Not everyone could afford to buy ice-cream at one anna. Upon receiving four such precious items, I wiped away my tears. I devoured the ice-creams with relish and fell asleep.

Did Bolpur Station have motor buses plying to Bolpur? I can't remember.

I only recall halting in front of Sri Bhavana. Before us stretched a long veranda (to my young eyes, that veranda appeared vast indeed). To the right of the veranda was the room of our 'Didi' or 'Super', Miss Boson. She was a French lady. We addressed her simply as 'Didi'—elder sister. Truth be told, I hardly addressed her at all.

To the left was Sudha-di's room.

Stepping into Sri Bhavana with Sudha-di, I forgot even to turn back for a last glimpse of my Baba.

Sri Bhavana of Those Times

It must be mentioned that as the Poush Mela came to an end in December 1938, my days there also ended. I had to come away to Kolkata.

I went back again to study for my BA degree. By then, the appearance of the buildings had also begun to change a little. At present, I'm talking about the three-year period from 1936 to 1938. From late 1944 to mid-1946, that was a different Santi-niketan. A grown-up perspective, seeing the place through new eyes.

Within the new itself, the old lived on. Today it seems amazing that it was sixty-four years ago when I first visited Santiniketan.

In the Sri Bhavana of those days, you went up the steps to enter a hall. On the upper walls of the front veranda, and inside the hall (by 'hall' I don't mean a very large room), there were frescos. A girl picking flowers strewn on the ground—that's the only image I can recall.

If any student received a visitor, that was the room where they were expected to meet and converse. By way of seating, the room had wooden asanas, long, rather high benches, ranged against the wall. They were upholstered in yellow handloom fabric woven at the ashram. To us, the main object of attraction was the hand-crafted double-storeyed doll's house made by Rathi-da (Rathindranath Tagore). It looked exactly like a real house. Sitting room downstairs with tiny chairs and tables, stairs leading up to the first floor. And upstairs, the bedroom, with furniture and bedlinen. That house even had a tiny light that came on.

I've seen Rathi-da make so many handcrafted things, at Uttarayan. I remember very well, just before the summer holidays in 1937 or 1938 (who knows if I'm right or wrong!), the marriages of Buri-di (Nandita) with Kripalani-ji (Krishna Kripalani), and Bishu-da, son of Mastermoshai (Nandalal Bose) with Baby-di (Nivedita), daughter of Tanay-da (Tanayendra Ghosh).

All the members of the ashram (including us) were invited, of course. On weddings and other such occasions at the ashram, the feast would be served in the kitchen. So we went to the wedding (we were taken there, that is). I observed that Rathi-da's gift was a bunch of large, white hand-crafted flowers, and there, placed on the petals, was a tiny golden bee. Was that Baby-di's wedding, or Buri-di's? I can't recall things in so much detail. But I do remember those petals swaying ever so slightly from the weight of the bee.

I meant to tell you about Sri Bhavana, but look how far I have digressed.

I followed Sudha-di like one entranced. In Sri Bhavana then, the central building was double-storeyed, flanked by a single-storey house on either side. Turning left immediately upon entering, and crossing the first chamber, one came to a long room with rows of beds. Students of Class Five, and probably also Class Six, all of us stayed in the same room.

At the centre of a mehendi hedge was an opening that led into Sri Bhavana. Then, moving forward, we climbed the steps.

Inside Sri Bhavana (from a child's perspective), one saw a large space enclosed by a wall. At one end of it were rows of bathrooms, and opposite, the toilets. Inside the bathrooms, a series of long choubachchas, water tanks built close to the wall. Santiniketan in those days suffered from a severe water shortage. As far as I remember, the supply of fresh water came at night. The water tanks would fill to the brim, then.

Outside, too, there was a large choubachcha. As Class Five students, we were placed under the supervision of several guardians. I have memories of Harani-didi, Kusum-didi, Golapi-didi.

After dinner, we would go to bed early, when it was still evening. It was an ashram rule that, at eleven o'clock at night, the power supply would be switched off. Our supervisors slept on the floor in our dormitory, and in a corner of the room, a lantern glowed all night.

If we needed to get up during the night, we would call out to our didis.

The problem was caused by wires stretched across the inner courtyard for drying the laundry. At one end, there was also a weirdly crooked date palm. Sometimes, the senior students would forget to take in their laundry. To visit the toilet at night, one had to cross that area. Then, those clothes on the line looked like bhutnis, and the date palm resembled a petni. How terrified we were, of those eerie female spirits!

Mira (Namita), a girl from Agra, was very clever. One day she instructed me:

'Go to bed with the name "Rama" written on your pillow, and all your fears will vanish.'

I actually wrote 'Rama' on the pillow, and, summoning up a lot of courage, dropped off to sleep. Now I think, how charming were those childhood days! How easily one believed in things, how little it took to shore up one's courage!

To the right of that inner courtyard, framed in the wall, was a door. Through that door and to the left, beyond a barbed-wire fence, were beds of tomato, lettuce, onions and other vegetables. Vegetables grew there, from the rainy season onwards, right up to winter. In summer, the underground moisture would dry up and the land would become parched. In the middle of that garden, mounted on a steel frame, was the ashram water tank. To the right, outside Sri Bhavana, was old Jaidev's little shop.

Later, in my college days, I didn't see Jaidev there. I heard that he had once suffered some sort of accident with fire. In Santiniketan, there was no end to this kind of hearsay. There was a girl who narrated a lot of mysterious tales with a tremendous air of authority. Jaidev's face was indeed partially burnt. How old he was, I can't say, but to my young eyes he seemed very, very old. That he was indeed very, very old could be proved by one piece of irrefutable evidence: he had witnessed Gurudev taking classes, it was said.

A simple, honest man he was. He used bundles of date leaf as fuel to boil the tea. Who consumed that tea? At the Santiniketan ashram, it was the rule to address one's seniors as dada and didi. Students of Kala Bhavana, the college and other such institutions were didis indeed. But even students of Class Seven were our didis. I don't think the girls and boys of Patha Bhavana drank tea those days. But some people certainly did.

Jaidev squatting in his deserted shop, kettle on the boil. In front of him, a sleeping dog, its tail curled up. I found this image as soon as I searched for it. There's a picture gallery in my mind, after all!

At Sri Bhavana, our beds had wooden frames fixed on them. At night, mosquito nets were compulsory. Next to the bed, close to one's pillow, was a table for one's books, notebooks, pencils.

That was the age of 'handle pens'. Wooden pen, nib to be attached when writing. One dipped the pen in the inkstand to write.

I feel sorry for you. You have never used a pen dipped in ink. There was a type of inkstand that didn't let the ink spill even if you tipped it over. At Santiniketan, we didn't graduate to the stage where you could use that type of inkstand. Whether we prepared ink from pellets dissolved in water, or whether ink-stands of that type were placed in the Sri Bhavana study rooms, I can't recall now.

In those initial days, my most miraculous discovery was the infinite beauty and distinctive aesthetic sensibility manifest in everything at Santiniketan. At Sri Bhavana, everyone's bed had a coverlet woven on the ashram looms, deep chocolate with saffron stripes, edged on both sides with a saffron border. In the storeroom, long, sturdy shelves where you placed your personal baggage. It was screened off with a saffron curtain. Brilliant saffron was the designated colour scheme of that area. In the same store, each girl student was assigned a giant saffron bag made of thick fabric. You stuffed it with your laundry, for the dhobi to collect. When you went to class, you carried your handloom mat, woven in the ashram itself.

And I remember gazing wonderstruck at the design of the buildings there. Forget about the structures in the Uttarayan enclosure—Konark, Shyamali or Udichi. Even the library, Sri Bhavana, Vinaya Bhavana for the Patha Bhavana boys, Singha Sadana—how beautiful they all looked!

Let me also explain why such unadorned beauty in the architecture and interior décor left me so wonderstruck. Did I tell you, or did I not, that the India of those days was ruled by the British? 1936, when I came to Santiniketan, was also the year that marked the Silver Jubilee of King George V. The houses of those times were built on a different model. I remember the house that Thakurda lived in as a magistrate in Mymensingh. It was a sprawling bungalow with enormous rooms and other such features.

Then came the move to Medinipur. The houses in Barge Town were beautiful. Thanks to Baba's exquisite taste, ours was the only house with curtains in Manipur handloom weaves, and bedcovers with uncommon patterns. When Boromama and Mejomama went to Bombay, they'd send Marathi saris for Ma and my mashis.

But the homes of the bigwigs there had sofa sets with upright backs. And inevitably, their walls were adorned with pictures of the Emperor of England. Because our house had none of those things, Baba was widely criticized by the residents of Officer Town and Barge Colony.

'I work for the government,' Baba would always retort, in response to their questions. 'But my wife doesn't, after all. The interior of our house is her very own empire, and I don't poke my nose into her domain.'

The architecture of Santiniketan in those times, the handwoven items of everyday use, hold no novelty when viewed from today's perspective. But at that time it appeared extraordinary. Gaganendranath and Abanindranath showed great esteem for cottage industries and indigenous arts. But Rabindranath himself, through the style in which he set up the place, contributed immensely to the transformation of Bengali taste. The design of those buildings, those curtains and bedcovers, had given my imagination a tremendous jolt.

Such taste was not commonly seen in the Bengal of those times. Gujarat was renowned for handicrafts and cottage industries. As late as 1953, the sight of lac paved interiors and rooms decorated with brass artefacts in Ahmedabad had captivated me. Now, even in Gujarat, such décor has become scarce.

Daily Wonders

In the Santiniketan of those days, all things filled one's mind with bliss.

Take, for instance, our daily routine during my residence in Sri Bhavana.

We had to get up really early in the morning. What a hustle and bustle! Roll up your bedclothes, fold the mosquito net perfectly. Spread the coverlet on the bed. I fold my mosquito net wonderfully well, even now.

What matter if somebody had brought fancy hair oil from home, or some good tooth-cleaning powder? (We had not set our eyes on a toothbrush then.) All that stuff lay packed up in our trunks. For us there were stocks of chalk powder, to brush our teeth. For our hair, pure coconut oil. There was no opportunity us to indulge in fancy styles. Harani-didi and her co-workers would comb and braid our hair.

'Always keep your hair tied up,' they'd instruct us. 'Else you will end up with a headful of lice.'

After brushing our teeth and taking a wash, we had to get dressed. At Sri Bhavana too, a bell was rung. We younger girls had to line up: Class Five in front, then Six. In this orderly fashion, we proceeded to the kitchen. Under our arms we carried books, notebooks and the mats for floor seating, our asanas.

Day or night, we used the rear entrance to the kitchen. Just beyond the door was a chaalta tree. In 1945, beneath that tree, flourished the shop run by Kalo. He sold tea, eggs and pyaraki (coconut-stuffed pastry made of flour, lovingly fried and steeped in sugar syrup. Food items, those days, had not reduced their size and weight to look like slim modern women). In my college days, I never went to class without stopping for tea at Kalo's shop. For by then I had grown addicted to tea. The first chapter in the narrative of Kalo's shop, which would later become so famous, unfolded under that very chaalta tree.

Walking in line, we entered the kitchen through the backdoor. The food was something to celebrate. In the morning, we had luchi made of atta, and mohonbhog that actually had raisins. Bhola and Hari kept calling out to us as they brought in the servings. They literally force fed us, with all that scolding. Sometimes we also had luchi with thick chholar dal or warm bondey. Or muri with bondey. The compulsory item was a glass of fresh, warm milk, which you had to swallow after the morning snack.

After breakfast, we headed for the early morning baitalik, for the hymn to be sung in front of the library. Every week, a different department would be expected to render the ceremonial prabhati songs, meant to be sung at dawn. Look how well I remember the songs we sang with such fervour when we were in Patha Bhavana!

— *Edin aji kon gharey go*

— *Pran bhariye trisha hariye*

— *Alo amar alo*

— *Bajao amarey bajao*

What enthusiasm, in selecting our songs! We had to learn those early morning songs of course. That process of learning became part of one's early days there. When some other group performed, we would listen with close attention. So what if we belonged to the infants' department at Patha Bhavana? Did that mean we would let ourselves be outdone by our seniors?

Baitalik over, we rushed off to class. All classes, of course, were held in the shade beneath the trees that grew in the space between Singha Sadana, Vinaya Bhavana, the library, and Dwarik (the hostel for older boys). Squirrels would descend from the trees to listen to our lessons.

The bell at Singha Sadana marked all the important moments. At nine in the morning, it rang to announce a short break. Then we'd rush towards the kitchen. In winter, we would drink fresh date juice. Or warm cocoa. And in summer, the yoghurt drink called ghol. Or bel pana, the juice of the wood-apple.

In my writing, I used the phrase 'daily wonders'. How true. The more I think about it, the more clearly I realize the truth of those words..

There were so many of us, people of so many different age groups, living in Santiniketan then. Staying away from home— there was cure for homesickness, after all.

But Santiniketan had taken full responsibility for our well-being. Different households have such diverse food habits. Santiniketan undertook to mould our minds, and our bodies as well. At breakfast we were encouraged to eat our fill. And again, at nine o'clock, a fifteen-minute break.

After that, we had to rush to class. On the way, one observed, daily, how the bark at the sal tree base had grown thick and fibrous. As if by night, Kinkar-da (Ramkinkar Baij) had come, sculpted the sal tree trunk at its base and gone away.

From the kitchen to our class, off we went. Along the way, you had a view of the mahua tree on our left, there beside the library. The tree bore flowers, and fruit as well. We'd pluck and devour the ripe, juicy mahua fruit.

Likewise, there was no end to all the amrul, ripe amlaki, bakul blossom, kheerkul (it grew behind the library; I never saw that type of tree again until I visited Rajnoagarh) and kul, that dropped off the trees into the dust, for us to collect and consume. We must have swallowed quantities of red soil and gravel as well. What if we did? You can look up the dictionary to learn about the variety of minerals required by the human body. Iron, zinc, cobalt, copper. So gravel is necessary too.

Going up the shallow steps of the library once more, at the corner on your left you could see the ishermul tree. Many years later, reading *Manasamangal*, I learnt that the pungent smell of the ishermul roots and blossoms wards off snakes. Ishermul was among the anti-snake trees planted on Santali mountain by Chand Sadagar in the famous legend. What a sharp odour the ishermul leaves gave off!

To our left as we headed for class was a large gate leading to the original or adi ashram and Mandir. It was topped by a bow-shaped iron arch. Inscribed on it was a Sanskrit phrase. I was told it meant: 'Where the world resides in one nest.'

But we are speaking of trees at present. At that spot, twined around the gate, you saw the tender green malati vine. I don't know if you all have seen the malati flower. In the rainy season, tender white malati flowers would blossom. Few flowers have such a sweet fragrance.

And then you got to class. Look at the way things were set up in Santiniketan! You attended class, and alongside, squirrels descended from the trees to listen to the lessons. These days, we constantly hear words like 'attentiveness' and 'work culture', but long ago, I had learnt to identify the creatures who remain constantly busy with their work.

From the age of about three, I used to observe ants with great attention. I don't know if you have read the epic about ants called *Lal Kalo*. But that only referred to red and black deon ants. Red and black suon ants, wood ants, the green-and-red poisonous ants that cling to the bark of the guava tree—I have observed them all. What a work culture they have! While one team heads north, always moving in line, another team heads south in a parallel line, directly adjacent to the first.

The squirrels at Santiniketan shared the same nature. Always busy. Always on the move, collecting and hoarding. Whatever they can get, they carry to their nest in the hollow of a tree and store it there. Those days, all of us familiar with the ways of squirrels knew that a squirrel's nest would yield many things that are not edible. Pencil stubs, used erasers, hairpins, a piece of ribbon—you could find all those things there.

'See how clever they are!' our classmate Biren Barua would exclaim. 'Putting together all that's needed for their children's education and for their daughter to braid her hair.'

Anyway, I'll talk about the living creatures of Santiniketan later. Like a crazy, derailed rail engine, I have left the main track and taken off on a different course.

So, as I was saying, we were supposed to attend class until eleven.

After class, the bell at Singha Sadana announced the end of morning lessons.

Now you had to run. Run towards Sri Bhavana. Put away your books and head for your bath. In Class Five, it was Golapi-didi and her co-workers who bathed us, massaging coconut oil into our hair, scrubbing us with soap in summer and mustard oil in winter. We combed our hair ourselves.

Then the bell rang in Sri Bhavana. Exactly as at breakfast time, we proceeded to lunch, walking in line. The youngsters were fed in the first batch. In 1936–38, I hadn't been promoted to the second batch, after all. That happened when I joined college for my BA degree.

Ah! Can I ever forget those meals in the kitchen? Benches and tables laid out for your meal. Thali, bowl and glass, placed before each of us. Hot rice, dal, vegetables. Large pieces of rui fish, cooked in gravy. After that, a bowlful of home-set yoghurt, rich and creamy, sweetened with sugar.

From among the kitchen army, I remember Bhola, Hari and Prabhakar.

'Khuku! Have some more rice,' they'd urge. 'Eat your fill.'

During my childhood days in Santiniketan, 'Khuku' was the name by which I was addressed most often. I don't remember anyone calling me 'Mahasweta'.

After your meal, a siesta for half an hour. Then, you got up for the study hour, in Sri Bhavana. An hour of writing. You completed your tasks in arithmetic.

Then, classes from two to four o'clock.

On the way back, we'd go into the kitchen. Every day, a different menu. Upma from South India. Or fried chire, flattened rice, with nuts. Enormous pantuas to go with it. Mango and banana in summer, oranges in winter.

Then, you put away your books and headed for the playing field in front of Sri Bhavana. Opposite the Sri Bhavana gate were benches beneath the luxuriant rain-trees that we called sirish. Beyond that lay the playfield. There we played ha-du-du, what we now call kabaddi. Ha-du-du we played, and gollachhut. From the following year, we also played hockey with the boys.

And then, dhong-dhong-dhong—the sound of the bell. Time to return to Sri Bhavana and take a wash.

I will always remember the evening prayer assembly.

I recall something of the language and intonation of the shlokas from the Upanishads that we chanted daily, standing in two rows facing each other:

> *Ya oshadhisu*
> *Yo vanaspatisu*
> *Tasmai devaya namo namah*

Calm, profound words of prayer. Their tones inspired awe in my heart. I would gaze at the trees. They were indeed vanaspati, divinities of the forest.

Santiniketan taught us to respect nature, and to love it.

After prayers, we settled down to study. Before that, Sudha-di and Nalini-di gave us a tumbler full of warm milk. Then one sat down with one's books. And after that, off to dinner.

The chaalta tree looked so friendly in the daytime, but at night I didn't dare even steal a glance at it. I felt too terrified. Yet there was no cause for fear.

'You read so many books,' Nalinidi would say. 'Don't you read ghost stories too? That explains your fears.'

We had unrestricted access to the library, though I never set my eyes on a book of ghost stories there. But I had read so many books in my own home, and anyway, my mind was ever-fanciful. Maybe those were the stories at work in my imagination.

Our evening menu was similar to lunch. Night or day, rotis were always served. At dinner we also had salad, and after our meal, a bowl of milk.

Back to Sri Bhavana after dinner. Now we became subjects of the kingdom ruled by Harani-didi and her companions. They'd check if we had washed and wiped our feet clean, braided our hair and hung up our mosquito nets properly. And in winter, as we shivered in the biting cold, they'd massage our feet with oil warmed in a bowl placed on the lantern flame. Into our beds we'd climb, tucking in the mosquito nets. And then, off to sleep.

I've recounted whatever I remember about our daily routine. Why did I tell you all this? In Rabindranath's time, Santiniketan offered independence. It offered nurture. And those days, they didn't teach us the value of discipline through any kind of preaching. They taught us through our everyday existence. That is the Santiniketan I summon up in my mind, daily.

That is where I learnt the endless joy of regular effort. Santiniketan also imparted a sense of responsibility and taught us to love and respect nature. It taught us other major things as well. I mean, they would plant in our minds the seeds of great philosophical ideals, like trees. The nature of these ideals I will reveal as I write this book.

Aldous Huxley says Rabindranath's major legacy lies in his thoughts on child education. Rabindranath transformed these ideas into reality. The list of all the worthwhile lessons he imparted to children is endless. He understood the profoundest truth and made it a reality. Yet, fifty-nine years after Independence, Bengalis have not understood the meaning of the word 'education', even now.

'Education' means building physical fitness by offering the body a balanced diet. And in order to mould human character, to train people to be active, efficient, free-spirited and confident, you must plant the seeds in early childhood itself. Train them daily, but don't let them realize that they are being 'trained'. Open their mind's eye. Let their inner eye learn to observe images, music, architecture, culture, beauty, all these things.

Today I understand these things. And I also understand that at the root of my becoming the person that I am now, lie the contributions of my family, my life after marriage—all those elements.

Those amazing three years of my childhood are also part of that process. Rabindranath taught us to be thirsty. Hence, I have learnt to drink life to the full with such avid thirstiness, to love nature and to remain free of narrowness. He also taught me to be self-reliant and independent.

Nobody speaks of Rabindranath's thoughts on child education. Because to speak, you need to think. And thought calls for action. We love words after all, not action.

Trees, Silkworms and Nature Studies

I must talk about our lessons in Nature Study. Speaking of nature involves talking about plants and trees, water and soil, insects and birds, even snakes and frogs.

Our Nature Study classes were compulsory. Just imagine! Nature Study was a compulsory subject in Patha Bhavana at Santiniketan, back then.

Tejeschandra Sen was our Nature Study teacher. To the right of the Mandir stood his extraordinary house 'Taldhwaj', 'House with a Palmyra Flag'. Why such a name? Built around a tal tree, it was a round cottage with triangular rooms made of clay. A thatched roof overhead. That was Tejes-da's home.

Tejes-da taught us to recognize plants and trees.

'Treading on the grass, do you realize that in a few days' time, silkworms will appear here?' he would tell us. 'Do you know how many yellow butterflies will be seen?'

How true! True indeed! After the Puja holidays, in the field before Sri Bhavana, hanging on every blade of grass, we found silkworms—we called them 'gutipoka'—all rolled up, tails and mouths conjoined. Now they had become pupae, enclosed in a casing. How dazzling the colours of that covering!

We were taught to procure boxes of soap from the Co-op, our ashram store. On Wednesdays we'd go to the Co-op with one rupee in hand, to buy pencils, oil and soap. Also needle and thread, and an anna's worth of toffees and lozenges. Sudha-di would dole out the money and give us our Co-op account books. We received four rupees a month as pocket money. But even for that amount, we learnt to keep an account. That was a lot of money, what you'd call excess, but only to be spent on necessities.

You pierced holes in those soap boxes. Collected silkworms and kept them there. Fed them leaves. New leaves each day. And tipping the box over, you discarded the old leaves and insect droppings (we called their excreta 'maath').

One day, you'd find the gutipoka all rolled up, tail and mouth together, hanging from the inner ceiling of the soap box. Then a shroud covered their shape. They had developed into pupae, in cocoons. We would say, 'they've tied themselves in bundles'. How attractive those bundles were! When they attached themselves to akanda, the swallow wort shrub, they looked like black Chinese lanterns. And the cocoons on the karabi, the oleander tree, looked like the Chinese lanterns of some fairy tale. Green dotted with gold. Pink. Pale yellow. What an exquisite display of colour!

In our young days at Dinajpur, there were all kinds of trees surrounding our house on three sides. My younger sister Mitul and I would gaze at such cocoons hanging from the karabi leaves.

'The fairies were here at night for sure,' we'd say to each other. 'They've left those lanterns strung up there.'

That's the problem with growing up, growing old. That karabi tree, those cocoons, that place called Dinajpur—if one spoke of those things, Mitul would say:

'Yes Didi, I remember.'

Now Mitul is gone. Gone are the two brothers born just after her. We were nine siblings. Now there are five, four sisters and a brother. The ones who are still alive are younger than me by many, many years. If I talk of my childhood, they won't understand.

During that same stint in Dinajpur, a tiger once entered the cattle enclosure of the farmers who were chor-dwellers, living on the sandbanks in the middle of the river. Baba had to clamber onto the thatched roof of the enclosure to kill that tiger.

The entire town probably boasted of one or two motor cars, no more. The dead tiger was paraded across town, displayed atop the roof of one of those cars. Mitul and I had gone out to watch.

'Didi!' Mitul asked avidly, 'Tell me, is that really a tiger? A real tiger?'

On realizing that it was indeed a real tiger, how frightened Mitul became, there in broad daylight, at eleven in the morning! She had to grip my hand tightly all the way home.

Anyway. Let me talk only about the silkworms of Santiniketan. For some days, the silkworm remained like that, all bundled up. Then one day, cutting through the shroud, a dazzling butterfly emerged. The first few instants, it waited, wings still folded, quivering. Then you carried the box outdoors, opened the lid and let the air in. In a trice, off it flew, taking wing effortlessly. Abandoning the transparent shroud. We had to perform this task with our own hands. Later, it became an obsession.

We were learning that different trees bred caterpillars that grew into butterflies of different types. From the silkworms that bred in grass and kalakasundey, you'd get tiny yellow butterflies. From an array of diverse plants—bel, shiuli, karabi, kalke, sal, ishermul, akanda, atasi—what a variety of cocoons we'd harvest! We grew quite competitive about the variety of trees from which we managed to procure cocoons.

It must be admitted that gutis from sal, shiuli and bel fruit trees were rarely to be found. From the sal-tree guti emerged butterflies as lovely as Nur Jahan, their dazzling white wings edged and dotted with gold. In size, much larger. Very few people succeeded in procuring gutis from sal trees. Butterflies bred in akanda shrubs were black, with red and white markings. Ishermul gutis also produced gorgeous butterflies.

Subsequently, I have taught my siblings and other youngsters to recognize and nurture cocoons. The silkworms that breed on the evergreen spring creeper madhabilata are wriggly creatures. They develop into moths, not butterflies. The gutis on spider lily plants look exquisite. But I think they too grow into moths.

What a wonderful life we enjoyed, then! Wandering with Tejes-da, learning about the characteristics, good and bad, of trees and plants.

On our way to the Mandir entrance was a baheda tree, shedding its fruit. We'd scrape the fruit with brick or stone to extract the kernel and devour it.

'Look, all these things have medicinal properties,' Tejes-da would inform us. 'All these plants and trees, shrubs and bushes, all the grasses that you see—were any of them created without a purpose, randomly? What invaluable qualities they possess!'

'Come on, taste some of these things!' he'd urge. 'Try some baheda! Savour the amlaki! No disease will invade your body, ever again.'

Savour those things we did, like herbivores, creatures of the wild. That probably explains why, to this day, I have rarely been afflicted by fevers and fits, stomach ailments or cold and cough.

We referred to amrul as 'sour-leaf'. How lovely those leaves! Like clubs in a suit of cards. You'd pluck and eat them at will.

And as for amlaki, it figures in song after song, story after story. Everything about raw amlaki, from its flesh down to its seeds, has curative value for a hundred thousand ailments. We'd shake the tree and devour the amlaki. Chewing, we'd feel a bitter taste in our mouths. Then we'd gulp water, and it would taste fine, rather sweet. Those of you who visit Santiniketan, gather from the earth the amlaki that has ripened on the tree, and taste it. Simply delicious, like the flavour of pickle on your tongue!

Mira Dasgupta, born poet that she was, would pose a query in verse:

Aam, amra, amrul, amlaki—
Jaam exists, jamrul too we see,
But why no jamra and jamlaki?

Why not indeed? We'd marvel at Mira's brilliance. What incredible talent!

On the stretch of land separating the library from the guest house grew gaab, mango, bakul, kheerkul and various other trees. A few guava trees as well. As for the amlaki trees, just don't ask about them. Scattered everywhere, those groves of amlaki, wild with the dance of leaves!

Speaking of chhatim trees reminds me of the Chhatimtola of those days, adorned by Debendranath's bedi, the platform where he prayed. I remember very clearly Rabindranath's lecture at the Mandir during my college days, and the book *Santiniketan* which I brought from the library (were there several copies?) to read in the shade of Chhatimtola.

That ancient chhatim tree, bent and gnarled with age, had spread in different directions. From gaps between the branches and foliage, we could see the main tree-trunk soaring up and branching out. But those branches were interspersed with hollows. Put your hand inside those hollows and you'll find bones, our seniors would say.

'Whose bones?'

'The dacoits who infested this area. Their bones. O baba! How scary!'

To students of Class Five, the boys and girls of Class Six seemed grown-up, and those of Class Seven or Eight seemed very grown up indeed. We believed literally everything they told us.

But we heard a ghost story just once. That too not directly from the teller, not first-hand, that is. It was probably the thirteenth or fourteenth adaptation.

I may as well tell you that story. Next to Sri Bhavana was an enormous compound. A pair of kadam trees grew in the part that flanked Kala Bhavana. Exquisite beauties they were, those kadam trees of ours. If you've seen a kadam tree, you will have noticed that the shape of the branches is very beautiful. When the trees blossomed during the rains, they appeared extraordinary. We'd gather and chew the fallen kadam fruit. The sour taste was delicious.

Beneath that pair of trees was a choubachcha, a paved water tank which remained empty. The choubachcha next to the Mandir also had no water. Water was scarcely available in Santiniketan those days, after all! It was due to the water shortage that we had a two-month summer holiday. Anyway, those kadam trees grew right outside the windows of the dormitory we occupied as Class Five students.

I have already told you about the marriage of Mastermoshai's son with the exquisitely beautiful Baby-di, the daughter of our English grammar teacher Tanay-da. Tanay-da used to cycle to Mastermoshai's house in the evening. Suddenly it was heard that Tanay-da had reported seeing, on his way home at night, a very tall figure leaning against the outer wall of our room. The figure had very long arms.

As the saying goes, the cow in a story can climb a tree. Who made up this particular story, for whose ears, and how the rumour spread, I can't say. But we were certainly terrified. We also knew the antidote for terror, though. Write 'Rama' on the pillow and close your eyes tight. The moment your head hits the pillow, fall into a deep slumber!

Speaking of trees, so many memories crowd the mind. I'll tell you more about those beautiful trees. Those deities who reside in medicinal plants and trees—the ones we addressed in our evening prayers—I salute all of them. I don't know about gods and goddesses. But as for trees, or any form of vegetation, they all serve the needs of this earth, after all. So, when I gaze at trees, I feel that all's well with the world.

Sometimes, when it rained, the short and roly-poly Tejes-da would watch the rain come down and tell us stories. The stories were probably meant for himself, not for us.

'Take the arjun tree. Can you tell me why the arjun is so famous?'

I was tactless and outspoken. Empty vessels make the most noise. With my meagre fund of knowledge, I used to talk too much.

'Arjun must have hidden his weapons in that tree.'

'Will you shut your mouth?'

I didn't snivel when Tejes-da scolded me.

'Arjun hid his weapons in the shami tree,' he informed me, patting my head with his thick, heavy hand. 'Shami is another name for the babla tree, do you understand? Arjun was no fool. The babla is full of thorns. He hid the stuff in its branches.'

'The wood of the babla is very strong,' added Dukkhaharan, a village lad. 'So is the wood of the tamarind tree.'

'Not only the wood, the babla tree has many beneficial qualities' Tejes-da said. 'Whatever Nature creates always has beneficial qualities.'

The babla tree has lovely foliage. The blossom looks like a tiny yellow powder puff. In our times, they used soft puffs to apply powder on infants' bodies.

'Whatever Nature creates has some form of value.' Tejes-da's words remain etched in my memory to this day. 'That's why, whenever I see plants or trees, I immediately wonder: What purpose do they serve?'

About sixteen years ago, somewhere near Mehrauli in Delhi, an elderly Rajasthani person had pointed out a babla tree.

'In Rajasthan, this tree is known as kalpabriksha, the wishing tree,' he told me. 'Camels devour its branches, thorns and all. The hanging clusters of fruit resemble broad beans. We use the seeds from those pods as fodder for our buffalos, goats and cows, to enhance their output of milk. And the wood has so many uses.'

'I know.'

'How do you know?'

'My teacher taught me these things when I was a child.'

For us, babla and pepe—our word for papaya—also served another purpose. They provided us with tongue twisters challenge each other with:

'Come on, say *babla gachhey baagh uthechhey* (a tiger climbed the babla tree)! Say it quickly. No pause, and no mistakes.'

'Then let's hear you say *kaancha pepe paka pepe* (raw papaya ripe papaya)!'

It's simply impossible to rattle off these words rapidly without making a mistake.

Everywhere, growing wild, we found the kalakasunde. Yellow flowers, fruits like borboti, the narrow bean, and the butterflies that bred there were yellow as well.

'Observe this plant, learn to recognize it. There's no saying how many ailments can be treated by its seeds, leaves and roots!'

Could we have learnt to identify the medicinal root called anantamul? It was Tejes-da who taught us to recognize it. The more we listened, the more we learnt from him about the benefits of plants such as anantamul, akanda, chhatim, hibiscus, banyan, bakul, baheda, neem, and dhatura.

'O Tejes-da! Earthworms are so revolting!'

'O re! The earthworm is the farmer's friend. Swallowing soil through its mouth, excreting it through its rear, it turns the earth, making it bator—ready for tilling at the right time.' Soft and moist. That's what 'bator' means.

Tejes-da addressed these creatures with the respectful pro-noun 'apni'.

'The esteemed earthworm consumes soil, and excretes it,' he'd say, using the formal, deferential mode. 'What are the hon-ourable birds doing now?'

'How busy they are!' he'd say in the same vein, using the respectful form of address. 'Eating the fruit and discarding the seeds, so new plants can sprout from them. See, likewise, how the butterflies hover, drinking nectar from flowers and scattering the pollen to extend the family of the flowering plant'.

Running about, we'd recite an entire alphabet of plant life. What you would call a quiz for children.

> *A-a-a!*
> *Ashok aparajita anantamul!*
> *Aa-aa-aa!*
> *Akanda akashnim amlaki!*

And so we chanted, as we ran.

Ah! How blissfully we spent our childhood days. What a magic spell was cast by the Santiniketan of yore! It was our infancy that taught us everything. It taught us to love the entire universe.

Why does education in love not feature in today's curriculum?

More about Trees

About the plants and trees of the Santiniketan that lives within my heart, I feel compelled to say more.

The neem trees will feel offended if I don't give you a proper account of them.

The neem trees that I know belong to three varieties. Akash neem, mahaneem and ghora neem. All three varieties blossomed in the warm month of Chaitra, and their fragrance filled the air. I saw the flowers, some white, some blue, but I can't say which type of neem had white flowers and which had blue. I can say for sure though that just in front of Sri Bhavana, beyond a spreading sirish tree, stood a row of neem trees, stretching right up to the end of the path. Today, the Sabars bring me neem honey and neem oil. And all year round, I consume boiled neem leaves.

In front of the Kala Bhavana flourished a 'jambuvana' or jamun grove. Why call it a grove? Because it was a unique type of jamun tree. Not the familiar high-crested black jamun, but low growing trees that spread their boughs long and wide. As far as I can recall, none of these trees grew even to the height of an ata tree. There was no dearth of fruit. Not too fleshy, the stone so large it felt like mango seed. Not too sweet either. But you could carry some salt wrapped in paper, and gorge on the fruits endlessly, until your throat began to choke on the bitter jamun sap.

Our entire cohort would invade the jamun grove together.

'What clever jamun trees, bhai!' Kitu (Krishna Roychoudhury) would exclaim. 'Not growing too tall. How easily we can enjoy the fruit.'

I've never seen such jamun trees anywhere else. They were just right for a place like Santiniketan.

Very profound, cheerful and large-hearted was the Ghantaghar, the bell tower, located beyond the library, to the right (am I correct?). A giant banyan or peepul grew there.

And other trees too: bakul, jamrul, gaab and sapeda. Close to Chhatimtola was a hapless tree that bore sour fruit which we knew by the name of 'nol'. That was the tree a boy from Garhwal (was his name Vinay?) tried to climb, when he slipped and fell, fracturing a bone.

The name 'banapulak' ('rapture of the forest') was given by Rabindranath to the tree that grew to the left of the path to Uttarayan. It bore clusters of blossoms resembling hasnuhana, exuding a sweet fragrance.

To the left, on the way to Uttarayan, the road had a culvert, and below, on a deep slope, was the house where Sebak-da lived—Sebak Sen and Jamuna-di. Mastermoshai's younger daughter Jamuna-di played the role of Kurupa Chitrangada in the first performance of *Chitrangada*. With her sculpted features, as if chiselled in black stone, she was exquisitely beautiful.

To continue what I was saying: in winter, beneath that culvert grew wild, flowering shrubs. In the month of Chaitra, those shrubs had dried up, but the ripe kul fruit still grew on every branch. Down I jumped, from the edge of the culvert, without a thought. Who was to know that, lying coiled under the bushes, was a hibernating gokhro snake? It was clear to me that all that stood between the snake and my feet was a kul shrub. I also realized that the coiled form was moving, beginning to unravel.

'Snake! Snake!' I shrieked.

The louder I screamed, I'm told, the entire bunch of Class Seven students shouted even louder:

'Snake! Snake!'

The boys reached out to me.

'Khuku! Grab our hands, bend your legs and clamber up!'

Thankfully for us, Sebak-da came rushing to the scene. (I think he taught us arithmetic.) Getting to the road, he yanked me up. And killed the snake as well.

And after that, a storm of scoldings! We beat a hasty retreat.

Near the rail tracks grew wild kul shrubs. Crossing the Khoai, we'd go in search of the wild kul.

At Uttarayan, on the wall of Bouthan's (Protima Devi) private garden, Rathi-da had painted a guava tree in playful strokes, styled exactly like the trees in Mughal paintings. A branch of the tree, twisted around and secured to an iron hook on the wall, looked quite wonderful.

To our eyes, the most miraculous flower was the yellow palash from Goalpara village. A pure yellow, like the atasi blossom. Later, in 1945, when Abanindranath was Vice Chancellor, we went to him once and found him gazing in rapture at a yellow palash flower placed in front of him. Between the Shyamali and Udichi buildings, did they later plant a yellow palash tree? I forget.

Rabindranath educated us in the idea of beauty in the design of houses. And beauty in naming a house—that too was a lesson to be learnt from him. Amiya Chakravarty's elder brother Arun died before his time. 'Aruni' was the name chosen by their parents for the house they built in Puri. I believe that Rabindranath's influence had something to do with it.

We saw birds. Birds of many species. In the years 1936–38, immediately upon entering Uttarayan, one saw an enormous room to the left with a metal grill in front. A pair of snow-white peacocks resided there. Someone must have gifted them to Rabindranath. When the rains approached, the peacocks would spread their fans and dance. That was a sight worth watching.

Santiniketan trained our vision. Learn to see, learn to see!

Chhabighar, the picture gallery, was located directly in front of the kitchen. So many pictures to be seen there! For a week they displayed a Chinese painting. The paintings were put up there by the teachers and students of Kala Bhavana. Then came a Japanese painting, then others. Everybody viewed them. In their comings and goings, they saw the pictures. Observing images is also something to be learnt.

I didn't learn. Thanks to Baba, right from infancy, we were used to seeing paintings at home. The *Jibansmriti* edition of those days carried a painting by Gaganendranath. I still recall the lines *jal parey pata narey*, and *daibadurjogey aparahata sei kalo chhatati dekha diyachhey*. After reading *Jibansmriti*, I went to Santiniketan. This impossible addiction to reading was the reason why I learnt to recognize life and the world through my experience of books. That is what I believe now.

In Patha Bhavana, Jadupati-da offered art lessons. Sometimes he took us to Kala Bhavana. From morning to evening, what a varied work schedule!

A work schedule, indeed! Identifying trees, raiding fruit trees, and in the rains, running towards the Kopai with Jiban-da and Sudhir Gupta-da, all of us getting soaked together, learning how to swim as we plunged about in those red, muddy waters during that downpour—these were forms of action, after all.

Every so often, listening to the baitalik songs at night, joining in the singing (was that in my college days?)—all that was action too.

Santiniketan taught us that there is no such thing as worthless activity.

Our Studies

Truth be told, I can't remember the books prescribed for study in each class.

I do remember that in our times, after Class Ten, we took the Matriculation examination, under the umbrella of Calcutta University. Our Matric was equivalent to your Secondary examination. You follow the Higher Secondary system, we had the Intermediate. And in 1946, after two years of study in Santiniketan, we took our BA examination there itself, but became graduates of Calcutta University.

What texts we studied, I can't recall. But in Class Seven, we read Rabindranath's *Pathaparichay* and *Rajarshi*. In the same class, we studied the history of different places, such as Egypt, Greece, Babylon, Rome and China.

English and Mathematics received a lot of attention. Arrangements were available for learning Hindi. We had two teachers, whom we addressed as Bare Pandit-ji and Chhote Pandit-ji. The latter was a highly erudite Hindi scholar named Hazariprasad Dwivedi. Generally, Hindi speakers opted for Hindi lessons if they so desired.

Much later, I heard people in Kolkata joke that, in Santiniketan, the students apparently play games in class and sing songs during their sports lessons. The mockery and ignorance stretched to such limits that in Class Eight, a girl from Beltola School used to taunt us:

'So, tell me bhai, is Santiniketan green in colour?'

I felt astounded. To this day, I remain puzzled at the very small number of Kolkata folks who came down for the Poush Mela in winter or the Basanta festival in spring! As if, precisely because of its proximity to Kolkata, Santiniketan was far too remote. On such occasions, one felt saddened. Why didn't anyone visit the place to see it for themselves!

Never mind, let that be. Let's talk about our curriculum. We studied English literature under the tutelage of Kshitish Roy-da, Sudhir Roy-da (elder brother of Bimal Roy the director) and Krishna Kripalani. All three were wonderful people. They gave us a lot of encouragement. With what care they taught us to write sentences created from our own imagination!

Alas, the occasion for writing this book has come at a juncture when, what with advanced age and the frustrating challenges of my activism, I don't get the time to write, and my memory also betrays me. Not that I don't write a lot. But what I write is 90 per cent non-literary; only 10 per cent can be described as literature.

Anyway. Tanay-da used to teach us English grammar. Tanay-da and (before marriage) Baby-di lived in a cottage in the inner courtyard of Binoy Bhavana. Tanay-da was dark, short and sturdy. His eyebrows I can't recall, but he had sparkling eyes. Personality so overpowering, we found him terrifying. His room astounded us. Thatched roof, and indoors, beneath the thatch, a canopy enshrouding all four walls, without any gaps. Any snakes that fell through the thatch would be trapped in that shroud. Tanay-da's attire, like everyone else's, consisted of a coarse dhoti and panjabi, both spotless white.

What class we were in at that stage I can't recall, but I remember an occasion when we were being drilled in English verbs, in their past, present and future tenses. Eat-ate-eaten . . . and so it went. I was sitting next to Pitambar. Both he and his brother Madhusudan were plump and extremely good natured. I was probably not bad at my studies, but there were many others like me. The Sindhi girl Padma Mansukhani, who joined us in Class Seven, excelled in English.

Well, Tanay-da was testing us in class. He'd announce a verb, and we'd have to provide the past and past perfect tenses. I don't remember who was sitting in front of Pitambar then.

'Think!' called Tanay-da.

'What comes after "think", Khuku?' Pitambar asked me.

'Think-thank-thunk,' I whispered in his ear, mischievously.

'Indeed?' Tanay-da exclaimed, when Pitambar repeated my words. 'So, would you rewrite the English grammar?'

'It was Khuku who prompted me, Tanay-da!' whimpered Pitambar.

Tanay-da let him off with a scolding.

'Bring!' he challenged me.

'Bring-brang-brung!' I pronounced, as if hypnotized.

As punishment, I had to kneel on the gravel.

I frequently had to kneel on the gravel. Only the utterly hopeless among us were chastised in this way.

All our classes took place beneath the trees. Only the Geography class was held in a room inside Singha Sadana. A map would be displayed, and using a wooden pointer, Sishir Mitra-da would identify every river, mountain or island. His table and chair were placed on a platform. Chalk and duster in the drawer. And the attendance register.

'Present!' we'd respond, when our names were called out.

Well, that was the season for catching the non-venomous hele or halhaliya snakes, flinging them at each other, and keeping them in our pockets. All over the ashram, as soon as they felt the touch of rain water, these non-poisonous, striped hele snakes would emerge. We, the boys and girls of Patha Bhavana, would catch them. Chucking them at each other gave us a great thrill. How did we summon up the courage to catch them? It fills me with wonder! Now, just thinking of it gives me goose-bumps.

I think it was in Class Six that this particular episode happened. All of us had taken great pains to capture hele snakes, stuff them in the desk, and shut them in. Sishir-da was rather tall. A handsome, good-natured man. He entered the class, stepped on to the platform and opened the drawer of his desk.

Out sprang the captive hele snakes, scattering here and there. What elation! Like prisoners set free! Why only snakes, all creatures are rational. It was reason that prompted their urge to get out of captivity. Poor things, they could be seen only for a brief period. Who knows where they disappeared after that!

What a tremendous yell Sishir-da had let out, on that occasion! All of us helped the snakes escape.

'Who is the culprit?' roared Sishir-da.

'Khuku!' responded the whole class, in one voice. Believe it or not!

I didn't get a chance to explain that this was the collective enterprise of the entire Class Seven cohort. For Sishir-da made me kneel on the gravel in front of Singha Sadana for the entire duration of the class.

Afterwards, it must be said, my classmates offered endless apologies. So, by lunchtime, we had arrived at a reconciliation. All this happened in the period between 1936 and 1938.

One day, in the hollow of a guava tree at one end of the mango grove, we discovered a bundle of hele snakes. Many snakes, entangled in a ball. We realized that rain was imminent. It was time for the snakes to wriggle about catching small frogs, but they didn't know it yet. Quickly, Ajit extracted the ball of snakes from the tree, and rolled it on the ground. The snakes shot off in all directions.

'Why such interference!' objected Tejes-da when he heard of the incident. 'The snakes know everything. When to emerge, when to move with speed, they know e—verything! And because they understand these things, they survive.'

In those three years at Santiniketan, I never heard of anyone killing a single hele snake.

We didn't kill snakes (later, in the years 1962–63, I was forced to kill a poisonous snake or two, but that's a different matter), didn't kill birds, didn't imprison squirrels. Our Santiniketan taught us to acknowledge Nature and its offspring.

'So many snakes, if each one killed humans on sight, would humans have survived?' Tejes-da often reminded us. 'Don't forget that.'

Now I find myself able to remember many things. So much that I've forgotten, so much that I remember. Tell, me, why do I remember the Santiniketan of our own times? Because I had stored those memories in my mind, that's why. My Didima used to systematically put away paper bags, strings to tie them up, and all such things. Because they would come in handy later.

'Those you look after will take care of you,' she'd say. Does the beauty of that saying need any explanation?

I often remember reading *Pathaprachay* and *Rajarshi* in Class Seven. As for the mode of instruction, you were expected to read, immerse yourself and retrieve for yourself the jewels embedded in the texts.

And you were expected to write.

How to write?

Let's say you had to create a composition in Bengali. So, why should the teacher inform you that 'Ashaadh and Sravan are the two months of the rainy season'? You had to write the piece yourself. Off to the library you had to go. Figure out what books you required. Ask for them. Read. The writing must be original.

And the library as it was then! How fortunate I feel to have seen so many things in a single lifetime!

On the first floor balcony of the library, white-haired Haricharan Bandyopadhyay sat cross-legged at his low desk, writing his lexicon, the *Abhidhaan*, on the sheets of paper placed there. How could I have known then, that one day I would purchase a copy of *Bangiya Shabdakosh* and remember that I had once seen this author at work on this very book?

Supreme in the library, above all others, was Prabhat-da (Prabhatkumar Mukhopadhyay). All that they say about him is true: handsome appearance, well-built and virile, dark beard and all. But we held him in awe.

There is reason to speak of 'awe'. In the Santiniketan of our days, the teacher–student relationship was wonderful. Even when we were frequently punished, asked to kneel, we felt our actions deserved such punishment.

But we couldn't behave informally with everyone. Tanay-da, Biswanath-da, Sudhir Gupta-da—we held them in awe. Prabhat-da, Kshitimohan Sen—we were in awe of them too. We kept away from them as far as possible. Most Wednesdays, Kshitimohan Sen would meditate in the Mandir. He had a distinctive personality. During my days in Santiniketan, I never heard any student dare to address him as 'Kshiti-da'.

In the library, our figure of inspiration was Satya-da (Satyacharan Mukhopadhyay). Satya-da would listen to us intently, and then select books for us. You read a book, then put it away, then wrote from your own imagination. In other words, you were expected to practice self-reliance in all matters.

I read two rare books in the library: Tejesh Sen's translation, *Kurono Chhele* (I don't remember the name of the original), and Priyamvada Debi's translation, *Kather Putul Panchulal*.

I remember them, even now I remember.

Nor was reading the only thing was required of us. We practised Bengali and English handwriting every day. We had to do sums as well. Our summer break lasted two months. For those sixty days, our homework included sixty pages of Bengali handwriting, sixty pages of English handwriting and lots of arithmetic. In Santiniketan, they never turned studies into a burden. They taught us to love even the effort of learning. That's why we did all the homework assigned to us with such alacrity.

All that practice in handwriting didn't help at all. Inscribed in my hand, (I'm a pen-wielding woman, not a computer user after all), some of the letters of the alphabet look atrocious. 'Ka', 'Pa' and 'Ba' look positively hideous. Never mind, it's no use dwelling on such things now. Didima, Thakurda, Baba-Kaka-Pishi, Mama-Mashi, my siblings, all of them excelled at handwriting. But as for Ritwik, Pratiti and me, our writing remains of an inferior order.

Our education didn't consist of reading and listening in the literal sense. In infancy itself, to sow in the mind's soil the seeds of a desire to learn, and to open the windows of the mind—such was the custom of the place I speak of.

Which is why, with a suspended skeleton displayed before our eyes, we were sometimes even trained in osteology.

'Look and learn,' our teacher would say. 'You'll learn, and also overcome your fear of ghosts.'

We viewed that skeleton on several occasions.

Again, when it rained, we were taught how to measure the rainfall. Such knowledge was considered essential.

'When you grow up,' Shailesh-da would say, 'I know you won't take up a profession that involves measuring rainfall. But what harm in learning?'

On the ground, we also created clay relief maps of the India of those days. Mountains, rivers, so many features seemed to spring to life. The India of our times looked different, indeed. Those days, even Bengal was undivided.

We learnt to weave at the loom with its clattering sounds. The boys learnt carpentry. Leatherwork, batik printing—we learnt a little of these things too. Just a little.

Let me conclude this chapter on education with the most narratable anecdote on the subject.

The year was 1938. We were in Class Seven. That year we heard that after many, many years, Rabindranath was going to offer a Bengali lesson to the tiny tots, and ours was to be the lucky group. In other words, it was our class he would teach. When the news broke, all of us seemed to grow ten feet tall. Our pride knew no bounds.

Our Bengali teacher Upen-da (Upendramohan Das) told us about the times when Gurudev gave Bengali lessons to Pramathanath Bishi and his peers, and when that period had ended. Upen-da was a very affectionate teacher. On the day I speak of, he was taking class. Meanwhile, the women labourers were at work, repairing the roof, beating it flat and singing in a low voice as they worked.

'All day I hear them sing about levelling the roof, as they work away at it,' Upen-da observed. 'Why do they sing?'

'We don't know!' we chorused.

'Well, listen then! Pounding the roof with that wooden durmush—there's a rhythm to it. Lifting and lowering it, all of them together. There's a tempo to that rhythm, as well. In manual labour, there's a rhythm and tempo, and the women are singing in tune with that. All human labour has a certain rhythm.'

Upen-da had a glass eye. He told us that during his childhood days in Comilla (?), they'd shoot arrows into the air from home-strung bows. Once, Upen-da's arrow shot far, far up in the sky, and he had raised his face to gaze at it. The arrow, on its descent, lodged in his eye. What agony we suffered, what terrible agony, listening to this tale!

Upen-da was very proud at the prospect of our going to attend class in Uttarayan. Only after the event did we realize that Uttarayan was the name for the entire compound. Upon entering the compound, the grand-looking house immediately to the left was named Udayan. Then came Konark, Punascha, Shyamali, Udichi.

We had always thought of Udayan itself as Uttarayan. That's why I say we arrived, armed with books and notebooks for the afternoon class, in the veranda of Uttarayan.

There was Rabindranath, on his armchair. Those who have witnessed it will know what that posture was like. Even during the hours of harsh sunlight, there in the veranda he would remain, motionless, seated in the same position. At that advanced age, he still had amazing control over his body.

Also present there, in the veranda, were Sudhamay-da, Anil Chanda, Rani Chanda, Anil-da's niece Juthika Dutta, and Upen-da. Most reassuring for us was the presence of Bouthan. Nandini alias Pupey, daughter of Bouthan and Rathindranath, was a simple, friendly girl. We would go to Pupey whenever we got the chance. Bouthan would always offer us something to eat. She knew that youngsters always have a secret craving for food.

The story 'Bolai' was the prescribed reading for that day's lesson.

Here I am, looking back in time. It is as if some shadowy photograph, faded with age, has again acquired a luminous brightness.

There was Rabindranath, on his armchair. And there we were, rows of us on a floor mat. He was reading aloud:

'My bhaipo, my brother's son Bolai . . . '

He read for a while. Then he asked us to speak. In response to his questions, we told him what we had understood from reading 'Bolai'. We all spoke, my classmates and I. Given a chance to speak, we always said a great deal.

What followed, I can't recall. But this episode was worth recording in the history notebook of our hearts, in invisible ink.

Of my peers—Mira Dasgupta, Namita Basu (Little Mira), Golap, Padma, Krishna, Ajit, Biren Barua, Pitambar, Swadesh, Jolly (then Anjalikumar Barua, later Abhijit Barua), and the others—how many are left now? Of those still alive, does everyone remember this episode?

I remember only this little fragment, after all. Diving into the ocean of memory and retrieving one water-soaked photograph after another, am I recounting all the details accurately?

Who knows?

Personages of That Era: Rabindranath

What names should figure here, and who can be left out? It is difficult to decide! How can a person poised to enter her seventy-sixth year on Poush Sankranti, travel sixty-five or sixty-six years back in time!

As for 'personages', I have encountered so many! Towering above all of them stands the figure of Rabindranath, whose greatness I am unworthy of measuring. Yet, the person who has prompted me to write this book remains very keen that I speak of some important personages. But it is difficult indeed to explain to him the ethos of Santiniketan in that era.

From Uttarayan to Gurupalli, and from the gate near Dwarik to Nilu-di's house—that was the total extent of the parameters of Santiniketan, in those days. (Nilima Barua and Nihar Barua lived in that house then. One sister, or maybe two. But we called it Nilu-di's house.)

Of course, beside the path leading from the front of Uttarayan towards Sriniketan, there was the house where Mira-di (youngest daughter of Rabindranath, mother of Nandita Kripalani) lived. And on the other side, the dwellings of Mastermoshai and

Rabindranath's brother-in-law. Indeed, there were all these houses. Still, the area was very small. Were there even 500 people, all told? I don't know. I studied in the infant division of Patha Bhavana, after all. At the age of ten, who knows such things?

Everyone was a member of the same ashram. So, I remember some figures more vividly. They were the ones with whom I was more closely involved.

Before speaking of Rabindranath, it must be pointed out that in my childhood, and thereafter, I addressed him as 'Gurudev'. Everyone did. But for a long time now, I have been referring to him as 'Rabindranath', so one has grown accustomed to that name.

As soon as I stepped into my twenty-first year, my life took a very different turn. That life was of another order altogether.

We youngsters had the license to go to Rabindranath. A very liberal license. And go we did. I remember very well the days when he resided in the house called Shyamoli.

In Class Seven, all of us developed a craze for autograph books. And spurred on by our history and geography teachers, we also acquired a keen interest in postage-stamp albums.

'Give us stamps,' we'd demand. 'You receive so many letters.'

Rabindranath would give us stamps. And hand us a candy lozenge each, as well.

'You too?' he'd say, when we held out our autograph books.

It's best to believe what I am going to narrate now. For this very episode will indicate the future course of my life.

When we went to Rabindranath, I sometimes gazed at him in silence and marvelled at the greatness of the person before me.

I had always seen Didima, Ma and the other relatives carrying Rabindranath's books. And Baba used to collect all the books that had Rabindranath's artwork on their covers: *Punashcha*, *Shyamali* and probably *Bichitrita*. Ma and Baba kept their Rabindranath collections in separate bookcases. I used to marvel at the number of books he had written. So many books?

In 1941, Baba bought me the English edition of *Crisis in Civilization*. That, of course, came at a later stage. But between 1936 and 1938, I can't even recall how many times I went to meet Rabindranath. He loved children.

Well, during that phase, I twice obtained poems embellished with his signature. Later, during my days in Kolkata, I was robbed of both notebooks. If anyone comes across those two poems anywhere, they should recognize that both belonged to my autograph book. It was due to my own stupidity that they passed into other hands in 1940 and 1947. The person who filched the autograph in 1947 was a well-known poet. A famous composer set the poem to music, and the song won great acclaim. Anyway, what use harbouring possessive feelings about something that is gone?

Today I think regretfully of my son Nabarun who never loses a scrap of paper, and preserves everything carefully. If I had given him those poems, they would have remained with us. Bijon was not disorderly, nor is Nabarun.

One of the poems goes like this:

Neel akashey brishtihara megher dal juti
Likhey dilo aaj bhuboney akaashbhora chuuti.

In the blue sky, clustered rainless clouds
Emblazon the news of a sky-wide holiday.

This poem was taken away from me in 1940.

The second poem:

Pathey jobey choli mor
Chhaya porey lutiye
Dharani kakhono tarey
Rakhey na to uthaye
Michhey khata bharo keno
Uro katha gulotey?
Mukti labbhuk tara
Miley jaak dhulatey.

As I tread my path
My shadow falls.
The earth never
Shores it up.
Why stuff your notebook
With useless words?
Set them free,
Let them mingle with the dust.

This poem went out of my possession towards the end of 1947. Surely someone, somewhere, has seen these two poems in print, bearing the Poet's signature? Today I have no regrets. The poems were once indeed in my possession. Today they are gone. My mind, these last 40 years, is unwilling to calculate what I did not receive from life. Because I have received so, so much. So much have I received, that the cup brims over, time and again.

Let me recount an extraordinary memory. Bankimchandra Chattopadhyay was born in 1838. In 1938, Rabindranath appeared at Chhatimtola, on the occasion of the Bankimchandra centenary, and delivered a lecture. I dimly recall that there were no outsiders present. Among the silent spectators, I too was present, part of the 'we' who attended. Now I realize how memorable that afternoon was.

But it was Santiniketan after all! If 26 June 1938 had not been a Wednesday (a holiday there), classes must have taken place on schedule. Even after that small commemorative gathering, we reverted to our daily routine. Our daily schedule was not to be forgotten.

That same year, preparations were under way at the ashram for the Barshamangal performance, to celebrate the rains. Our minds were intoxicated by the easterly monsoon breeze. The Sangit Bhavana of those days consisted of a large room flanked by two medium-sized ones, beneath a tin roof.

Sailaja-da (Sailajaranjan Majumdar) accompanied us on the esraj as he trained us to sing *ei sravaner buker bhitor agun achhey*. Our chorus was singing in full force. It was also raining heavily that year.

At that juncture, Biru-da (was his name Bireswar?), son of Gosain-ji (Nityanandabinod Goswami), came down with typhoid. Not only then, but even in later times, until the discovery of antibiotics, everyone would say:

'People don't survive typhoid. If it strikes when you are young, the disease is even more deadly. Your illness may be cured, some part of the body becomes paralysed.'

Biru-da down with typhoid, a pall of gloom enveloping the entire ashram. Then one rainy evening, Biru-da passed away. A black vehicle emerged from Uttarayan and headed towards Gurupalli. After a while it came back.

The alarm bell at Singha Sadana rang dhang dhang dhang dhang dhang. Five times. A pause. Then, five times again. The alarm bell resounded with urgency. Summer or winter, it would ring if a Santhal village caught fire. The ashram dwellers would rush to put out the blaze.

Did the bell announce the tragic tidings of a death or other such mishap? I dimly remember that it rang three times with pauses. Or once, with pauses. Was it so? Or maybe it didn't ring at all. Jayashri (Chanda/Sen) affirms that the bell did ring five times, with solemn pauses in-between.

We agreed that at the core of that monsoon month of Sravan, there was indeed a burning fire, as in the song we sang. It snatched away Biru-da, didn't it?

Large eyes, exuding health and vigour, how old Biru-da was at that time, I don't remember. That was either 1937 or 1938. After so many decades, is it an easy task to write from the blurred memories of what happened so long ago! Can the one who impels me to write, narrate his own recollections of the time when he was eight years old?

I remember quite well that many new rain songs were composed that year.

Such as:

>*Mon mor megher sangi*
>My mind is the clouds' companion . . .

>*Sravaner pabaney akul bishanna sandhyaye*
>This melancholy evening,
>>tormented by the Sravan breeze . . .

>*Ei sravaner buker bhetor*
>In the heart of this Sravan season . . .

Esho shyamal sundar
Come, O darkly beautiful one . . .

I'm sure I have made some errors. That is very possible. But it is a fact that Sailaja-da taught us one rain song, terrifying as a deluge, sweeping you away with its force.

This is how it went:

Aji borishar rup heri manaber majhey
Chalechhey garaji, chalechhey nibir saajey.
Hriday tahar nachiya uthechhey Bheema,
Dhayitey dhayitey lop korey choley seema.
Kon taronay megher sahit meghey
Bakkhey bakkhey miliya bajra bajey.

Behold, the beauty of rain in the heart of humanity!
Roaring tide, surging forth, in dense, dark attire.
Bheema's heart explodes in dance,
Torrent unstoppable, breaking all bounds.
What drives cloud with cloud to clash,
Chests colliding, to crashing sounds of thunder?

I'm sure that I am misquoting. It is only to be expected. But the profound, oceanic pulse of this song still haunts my memory.

In the 1960s, I bumped into Sailaja-da somewhere.

'So, you're writing. That's all very well. But why did you give up music?' That was the first thing he said.

How to tell him that I haven't given up music? That I sing many songs to myself?

'It's so sad that I don't get to hear the song *Barashar rup heri*,' I replied.

'That song? *Nachia uthechhey Bheema?*' he responded at once. I nodded.

What a man! In his last days, he sent someone—a favourite student, disciple or researcher—to record part of that song in my voice, on a cassette.

Anyway. On account of Biru-da's death, Barshamangal was not celebrated that year. The ashram troupe accompanied Rabindranath to Jorasanko. On the stage of Chhaya Cinema, in his presence, the Barshamangal performance took place. In that show, I too participated in a children's chorus number.

'When we went on stage, someone pointed at you and said: "That's Manish's daughter,"' Subodh Sengupta would always recall.

I don't remember that journey to Kolkata. What I remember is the extraordinary rapture I felt within. As if we were entering the magic realm of fairy tales. So, this was the fabled Jorasanko!

Of that occasion, I recall only the recitation of *Hriday amar nachey re* in Rabindranath's voice, accompanied by the Kandyan (Sri Lankan) dance performed by Santi-da (Santidev Ghosh). Cowrie-shell necklaces, adorning his chest. Santi-da, muscular, handsome, vibrant. And his dance.

Since Buri-di (Nandita Kripalani) and Mamata-di (Mamata Bhattacharya/Dey) had come there, they must also have danced. Many songs were performed as well. But I have forgotten everything.

Rabindranath himself, attired in undyed garad-silk dhoti and panjabi, performed the early-morning prayer ritual at the Mandir on the seventh day of the cold month of Poush. And at the Bhadrotsav festival in the rainy season, I also witnessed the evening prayers at the Mandir, with the glow of candlelight all around us.

All this I saw, and from so close! I didn't realize then, that not everyone is so lucky!

In that same three-year period, the dance dramas *Chitrangada*, *Parishodh* (later *Shyama*), *Chandalika* and *Tasher Desh* were performed. Rabindranath oversaw the rehearsals for a long time. What happened there, we can recount later.

I'll certainly share more memories of Rabindranath during that period. I'll say much, much more. But there are so many other faces knocking at my heart, I have no choice but to open the door to them. No, let me first finish what I was saying about the subject at hand.

The dance dramas only emerged in the public domain after receiving their release order from their creator. The poet travelled to Bombay and other places, where these dance dramas were performed. Afterwards I learnt it was to raise funds for Santiniketan that these plays were staged. So I was told. But wherever Rabindranath went, people felt honoured to set their eyes upon him.

In the final stages of preparation, rehearsals continued in the Uttarayan hall, day after day. We youngsters from Sri Bhavana also went there to watch. We sat through the rehearsals, motionless, like dolls. We were allowed in because Rabindranath wished it so: that was clear. Otherwise, for us to watch rehearsals during our usual study hours would have been impossible. Such things didn't depend on our own wishes after all!

Through the rehearsals, Rabindranath remained in his armchair, so utterly still! Who could tell that he was seventy-eight or seventy-nine years old! Ever since I learnt, from reading *Jibansmriti*, that he walked a lot, stayed up late and climbed the Himalayas in his early childhood, I became convinced that these were the factors behind his immense physical resilience. Nobody made the slightest sound during a rehearsal. And if there was the minutest slip in the dancing, singing, tempo or rhythm, Rabindranath's gaze would signal its occurrence.

Do you know what was our most valuable gain in all this? Rehearsal over, we'd head for that shiny oval table at the foot of the staircase leading up to the first floor. Rabindranath took the head of the table. And placing us youngsters from elementary school at the other end of the table, Bouthan would feed all of us. I have never seen such an affectionate, tender person as Bouthan. She wore silk saris in soft shades. The end of her sari, half veiling her head, would never slip an inch. In winter, sometimes, she wore a shawl.

I never saw Rabindranath overeat. Bouthan would serve him his food. And we would devour an elaborate feast, replete with all sorts of delicacies. Afterwards, we'd head back to Sri Bhavana. Yes, we Shishu Bhavana students dined at the same table with Rabindranath himself. No wonder I feel I'm writing a fairy tale!

The first performance of *Chitrangada* was staged before the summer holidays, in the outer veranda of Uttarayan. The backdrop was made of black fabric. That was probably in 1936. I think some people came down from Kolkata for the show. All of us from the ashram were present.

O ma! Just as the performance was about to begin, what a tremendous storm broke! The fiercer the storm, the wilder the whirl of falling leaves. Ultimately, the play was staged inside the

Uttarayan hall. On that occasion, Baby-di played Arjun, and Jamuna-di was Chitrangada. Buri-di was cast as Surupa, the beautiful version of Chitrangada. Hasu-di, Anu-di (I forget their proper names), Mamata-di, Anita Barua (later Grewal) and some others I can't recall, performed as sakhis, Chitrangada's female companions.

At the end of that performance, Surupa Chitrangada declared:

O Kounteya!
Driven by desire,
The sakhi offered up to you the gift of all her beauty!

Subsequently, those lines in verse were set to music.

What I'm doing here is foolhardy. Writing away from memory. If loads of errors come to light, let them. There's nothing I can do about it.

During that time, watching those rehearsals, watching that performance, we'd keep singing *Rodan bhara e basanta* or *Elo elo elo re dasyur dal*, whatever song we liked, whenever we wished.

Immediately after *Chitrangada* came *Parishodh*, later named *Shyama* (?). I seem to recall that in the dance drama *Parishodh* as well, Baby-di played the lead as Bajrasen. But in the first performance, who played Shyama—Buri-di, or Mamata-di?

We swooned at the sight of the dancers. Mamata-di, granddaughter of Jagadananda Roy, was exquisitely beautiful. Those days, to reach her house, you crossed the field in front of Sri Bhavana, to arrive at a pond or reservoir. Beyond it stood the single-storey home of Mamata-di and her family. Jagadananda had passed away. Mamata-di was fatherless. Her elder sister Susmita-di was already married. I never saw their mama Patal-da exchange a single word with anyone. But many rumours flew about. Such as the story that Patal-da sometimes went out, striding at great speed, lantern in hand, in that blazing heat. Whatever we heard, we believed (because it came from grown-ups), and gazed at him in wonder.

When they went touring with the troupe of dancers, how eager we were to see what they'd buy from the co-op! Hasu-di, Mamata-di, buying fragrant hair oil, or scented soap! As if they were off to the land of dreams. When the troupe travelled to Bombay, Sejomama, Hiten Chowdhury, and a few others gave their heart and soul to ensure the success of the dance dramas.

One spring, at the Gouraprangan courtyard, in the light of the Basanta full moon, Mamata-di had danced to *manohara bandhanam* with captivating grace. The performance took place in Rabindranath's presence.

Chandalika was distinctly different. Mrinalini Swaminathan (later Sarabhai) played Prakriti's mother. Her tall, lithe frame, and the dancing, different from the Manipuri style, had given the performance a new dimension. I liked *Chandalika* best of all.

And then came *Tasher Desh*. At those times, with preparations under way for each of the four dance dramas, I watched rehearsals, dined at Uttarayan and saw the legendary Rabindranath at such close quarters! Just imagine!

25 Baisakh falls on 7 or 8 May, during the summer holidays. So before the summer break, the ashram members celebrated Rabindranath's birthday, at dawn, in Amrakunja the mango grove. We little ones occupied the front row.

I don't know if any other school paid such close attention to infants. Maybe, maybe not. But in Santiniketan, children's education was an entirely different matter.

At this point I must recount some of my matchless exploits. But before that, let me say that as I write, I marvel at Rabindranath's qualities. How did his creativity continue to flow with such full force, right up to the end? What lessons he offered to the land and the people, throughout his life! At the festival of his creativity, children had an open invitation. What a great thing that was! And then again, teaching us to take responsibility for the well-being of infants. I remember, I remember all this very often.

Anyway, let me narrate the story of my matchless deeds. That also happened when I was in Class Seven. Before some holiday. We were to enact *Lakshmir Pariksha*. I was to play Kshiri, with Seba (Maiti/Maitra) as Rani Kalyani, Anima-di (Mira Dasgupta's elder sister) as Lakshmi. Because I was brash, I was cast as Kshiri. Seba the limpid beauty, a very mischievous girl, was assigned the role of Rani Kalyani. Seba was a year senior to me in school but I didn't call her 'didi'. It was unthinkable. Anima-di was also very beautiful, in a sweet and gentle way.

Anyway, the rehearsals went on and on. And then, of course, we had to practice in Uttarayan. Rabindranath would oversee the final stages in person.

So we went there. After watching my performance for a while, Rabindranath realized I wasn't getting anywhere. How to deliver the lines about 'Bhola Moira's wickedness' with the right gestures, he tried to demonstrate several times. And so it went on, for a few days.

Then came the day of the performance.

Suddenly I lost my voice.

Probably it happened because I'd been rehearsing my lines at the top of my voice. On the day of the performance, Buri-di made me gargle with salt water. She also plied me with doses of onion juice. And she kept up a torrent of scolding.

In the end, we managed to pull off the show somehow.

That was the first 'sadventure' of my acting career.

On the second occasion, a comedy by Rabindranath was staged. Mira Dasgupta played the husband, attired in dhoti and panjabi, a moustache drawn on her upper lip. I was probably cast as the quarrelsome wife. I wore a sari, with a hair-knot on top of my head, and wooden sandals.

After the performance, we were racing to Sri Bhavana. The boys in our class were giving us chase. We were running. All this was an expression of our exuberance. In front of the kitchen was a heap of gravel. Running, I tripped and fell, and Mira-di, who also stumbled, fell on by back.

Then followed a flood of sympathy. The next scene: there I was, in Sri Bhavana, seated with my legs dangling. Enter Doctor Babu, Senior. Also present was a Doctor Babu, Junior. Supplies of warm water, cotton and tincture of iodine, brought to the scene. Doctor Babu, removing the dust from my wound with cotton soaked in water. Extracting the gravel embedded in my knee, the blood flowing freely. Steeping the cotton in iodine, he pressed it down on the wound and bandaged it tightly.

Both my legs carry some marks of that 'sadventure', for sure!

At home or in the ashram, we dealt with minor injuries by chewing on tender grass or marigold leaves or applying their juice to our wounds. Iodine was not used in all cases. On that occasion, though, I clearly remember returning home with bandages on both knees.

The person for whom I am writing this book wants me to recount my 'interactions' with people. But I haven't succeeded. In the remote past, what conversations I had and with whom—can I remember all those things? And since I was a child, it's the people who were constantly around me and the ones I met regularly, who are likely to surface most vividly in my memory if I try.

For instance, I remember the kitchen and Sarojini-didi very distinctly. From age ten to twelve, in those three years of my life, the kitchen played a major role, after all!

Then there was Mallik-ji, as we called him. I think his name was Gurdial Malik. He hailed from the Punjab. About him, my Chhotomama, Sankho Chaudhuri, can tell you more. At that time, and for a long time after, Chhotomama lived in Santiniketan. He had a profound connection with the ashram. He was not only Kinkar-da's pupil, but also had a deep bond with the sculptor. If we had asked Chhotomama to edit this book, he could have filled many of the gaps in it. He could have reminded us of many forgotten names. But that was not to be.

About Mallik-ji, Chhotomama knows more. I remember the song Mallik-ji used to sing at dawn:

Utho jaago musafir bhor bhayi
Ab rainu kahan tu sovata hai . . .

Bhor bhayi—what an exquisite expression! Chhotomama can still sing this song. Mallik-ji was not too tall. A sturdy, fair complexioned, elderly man with greying hair and beard. How long he remained in Santiniketan and when he left, I can't recall.

I have seen Andrews-saheb. The title 'Dinabandhu' suits him indeed. Andrews-saheb with his hoary locks, heading for Uttarayan, dressed in panjabi and pyjama—I recall that image very vividly.

As for Cheena Bhavana and Hindi Bhavana, I have watched those structures being built. Mastermoshai at work, creating frescoes, along with students from Cheena Bhavana and Kala Bhavana—that, too, I have witnessed. Nobody told us then that what we were witnessing was the stuff of history. Mastermoshai went about, wearing his glasses, appearing totally self-absorbed. During our art classes with Jadupati-da, Mastermoshai would walk past, and sometimes drop by to take a look at our work.

Kinkar-da with his shaggy, knitted brows, always smiling. The statue in front of the guest house had been completed by then, or perhaps it was in the making, I can't quite remember. Many things happened, about which we heard from our elders. In winter, when the light had barely dawned in the eastern sky, Kinkar-da, wrapped in a blanket, would set forth for a drink of fresh tal juice. Sometimes, Mastermoshai would also do such things, we were told.

Once, spotting someone atop the tal tree, Kinkar-da took him for Mastermoshai, and Mastermoshai assumed it was Kinkar-da. When the two came face to face, they realized that the figure on the tree was some third person.

'Hey! Who are you?' The one who responded to their shout with an angry grunt turned out to be a bear. True or false I can't say, but we used to hear such stories.

Binod-da (Binodebihari Mukhopadhyay) with his near-blind eyes—what wonderful pictures he painted! We'd gaze in awe. A famous person indeed! But to our eyes in those days, no one appeared as 'a famous person'. Like hundreds of thousands of people, I too grew up knowing the name of 'Rabindranath'. But even to him, we enjoyed such easy access.

I have already recounted how afraid we were of Kshitimohan Sen. Short, curly, jet-black hair, snow-white complexion, what a tremendous personality! He regularly offered prayers at the ashram, and the glass hall resonated with the sound of his voice.

Prabhat-da was someone we held in high esteem those days. He had been brought up by Mohor's father, Satya-da.

Santi-da, Sailaja-da, Buri-di, Kripalani-ji, all these were people we recognized by the very mention of their names. The local people were fortunate to have Santi-da with them for a long time. I visited Santiniketan for the Poush Mela centenary. To share the stage with Santi-da—could I ever have imagined such a thing? That was the year when Amita-di (Amita Sen) invited me to her house and fed me with so much affection. In our childhood, in our mental geography, all these people belonged in the ranks of the senior and highly revered.

When I was in Patha Bhavana, Chhotomama was studying for his BA degree. It was his classmate Baladev Grewal whom Anita-di later married.

Some Other People

Without speaking of Sarojini-didi, this account won't be complete. Widowed after the birth of her only son, she may be described as the general manager of our kitchen. A diminutive figure, with a wrap thrown across her shoulders, over her plain widow's garb. Sombre by nature, but ever-alert to ensure that the kitchen remained an ideal place for meals.

The menu was well regulated. On Wednesday, our weekly holiday, meat would be served. And the habishyanna prepared on the seventh day of Poush, was famous indeed. During the winter festival in the month of Poush, the girls had to help prepare the sweets called pithe. But on 10 March, when Gandhi Divas was observed, all the workers at the ashram had a day off. I remember being part of the team that cleaned the toilets. On that day, all the work was handled by ashram dwellers.

Who did the cooking on that occasion? I must admit that I can't remember.

Then Sarojini-di's son got married. The arrival of her daughter-in-law, our Boudi, made her empty home replete.

I left Santiniketan in 1938 and returned in 1944, as a college student studying for my BA degree. Sometime in the intervening years, Sarojini-di's son died at his workplace. His daughter probably never saw her father.

In their home the two widows, and at the ashram that little girl, the apple of everyone's eye. Was her name 'Alo', the word for light? I can't remember. She was constantly passed around, carried in the arms of various people. Once, someone took her along to Bolpur. On the way back, the infant was killed in a road accident.

When I joined college, Sarojini-di was still around. Spine stronger than a thunderbolt. She handled all the work and saw to everyone's needs. Why some people suffer so may blows of fortune, I have never been able to fathom.

Returning to Santiniketan as a college student, I found Hari, Bhola and Prabhakar still working in the kitchen, just like before. One of them won a large sum of money in a lottery. What he planned, or did, with that money, became a subject of hot speculation in our circles.

About All of Us

At Patha Bhavana, I got to know Mohor. And in college, Suchi-tra. In our younger days, Mohor and Seba (Maiti/Mitra) were close friends. They were probably a year senior to me. Even at that time, Mohor was an exquisite beauty. She would come dressed in her deep-blue handloom sari, neatly draped. She did not need to apply kajal. Her eyelashes were as lovely as her eyes.

Seba, her elder brother Ashis-da, and later her younger sister Pushpa—all of them studied in Santiniketan. Seba was the naughtiest girl in Patha Bhavana. Very charming, with curly hair cascading down her back. On Wednesdays, in Sri Bhavana, the floor of our room became the stage for our theatricals.

Under Seba's leadership, we broke into the ashram garden behind Sri Bhavana, parting the barbed wire to climb through the fence. For such antics, the afternoon gave us a long stretch of time. Filling the gathered folds of our frocks, we stole tomatoes, lettuce, green chillies and onions. And later, squatting on the terrace, we prepared a mixture of all these ingredients and ate it with great relish. Even in those early times, Seba was a wonderful dancer. In our college days, I have watched her perform as *Shyama*.

Mohor, right from then, had the voice of an angel. Even when she was tiny, everyone already knew she was destined to be a singer. We used to visit their house as well. In Gurupalli, everyone lived in houses built of earth, roofed with tin or thatch. Mohor was the favourite daughter of the house. She and Seba were very fond of each other.

At Sangit Bhavana, scholarships were introduced in 1938. The recipients were the Sindhi girl Bishni Jagasia and my Chhotomashi, Swapnamoyi Devi, my mother's younger sister. Chhotomashi joined in 1938. Her stint at the ashram was truncated, as she was married off in 1939.

Bishni was a limpid beauty. From Burma came Sandhya Guha and Madhavi Guha. Madhavi, or Bunu as she was called, was a year junior to me. Both sisters were pretty, but in different ways. Bunu could be described as a bullet, she was so restless. I recall that Sandhya-di knew how to perform the poye dance and possessed the costume as well. Once, at the Barshamangal celebrations, Bunu danced in the Library veranda, to the song *esho shyamala sundara*. And Banalila-di, daughter of Gujarat, danced to the song *oi malatilata doley*.

In this fashion, students arrived in Santiniketan, from so many different places. From what we call Sri Lanka today, then known as Ceylon. Ceylon, Madras, Kerala, Gujarat, Maharashtra, Punjab, Karnataka, Manipur, Assam, Tripura, Bihar, Himachal, UP (today's Uttar Pradesh, then named the United Province). In fact, students even came from Java and Bali. In Patha Bhavana itself, my fellow students included Golap Srivastava from Bihar, and Gul and Padma, the boy and girl from Sindh.

At the very outset of this narrative, I mentioned Rabindranath's two major contributions to elementary education, of immeasurable importance. First, coeducation, right from infancy. From Patha Bhavana to Siksha Bhavana (college), Sangit Bhavana, Kala Bhavana—everywhere, for boys and girls, there was coeducation.

As for the second aspect of Rabindranath's thought, we realize today how essential it was. From their very infancy, boys and girls from diverse regions (states, in today's language) and language backgrounds studied together. As a result, no provincial narrowness ever entered the mind. Unconsciously, we absorbed the understanding that all of us were citizens of the same land, our Bharat. Citizens of this world, we might say, considering that students came there from Java and Bali as well. Studying in Patha Bhavana at Santiniketan, it was inevitable that our minds should absorb the awareness that the entire world and universe could be found there, in a single nest. Such was the imagination of the creator of the ashram.

These are the things I consider my greatest gains. It is a matter of deep regret that even after receiving so much, the country has not been able to realize in concrete terms Tagore's ideals of child education. Had we tried, we could surely have created a few residential educational institutions on the soil of Bharat.

My seniors, who are still alive, will surely remember those days in Patha Bhavana if they had studied there. Even in the post-Tagore age, many former students would remember these things. When we meet, we speak of the period between 1944 to 1946 as well. It is to be expected that within the heart of each individual a personal notion of 'our Santiniketan' must have survived. If not, that will be a great pity. If the memory has survived, then they can close their eyes and rinse their hearts in that pensive, free-ranging breeze, redolent of sal and neem blossom.

Festivals and Seasons

Tell me, what should I say about festivals? The festivals of today must have been celebrated in those days as well. We too were present at all those festivals, for sure!

Though we never went there, we heard of the Saraswati Puja at Goalpara village. The senior boys used to attend. So this is based entirely on hearsay!

Baisakh, Jaistha, Asadh, Sravan, Bhadra, Aswin, Kartik, Agrahayan, Poush, Magh, Phalgun, Chaitra—those are all the twelve months on the Bengali calendar.

Why 25 Baisakh could not be observed on that exact date is something I have already explained. In the month of May, water at the ashram was in scarce supply. Hence, the poet's birthday used to be celebrated in advance in the mango grove, through dance, music and poetry. Attired in snow white dhoti and panjabi, he'd alight from his vehicle. How dazzling he looked! His appearance lit up the mango grove.

In the monsoon, we celebrated the festivals of Halakarshan and Barshamangal. The Palli Kalyan Kendra (I've got that name wrong) was in Sriniketan, as the poet would later name the place. It was located in Surul.

Rural development is a necessity. Reportedly, it was from this conviction that Rabindranath inspired Rathi-da, Santosh Bhanja, Kalimohan Ghosh and so many others to devote themselves to this task. Kalimohan Ghosh was the father of Santi-da and Sagar-da. Kali-da (I never addressed him as Dada, never had the opportunity) had a sturdy physique. He used to move around on a bicycle.

I had forgotten the dates of the Surul Mela. Now, Kalyani (Das/Roy), my friend from college, informs me that it used to be a three-day fair, held on the fourth, fifth and sixth of February. What a relief to be reminded of this! I recall that in our college days we went to the fair with palash blossoms tucked in our braids. Since it was the month of February, some palash trees would have begun to bloom.

Once, when I visited the Surul Mela as a child, Chhotomama was roaming about with Haren Ghosh. Through Haren Ghosh, Bani Majumdar (elder sister of Shanu Majumdar/Lahiri) had come to the ashram after training in the Chhau dance at Sarai-kela. Rani-di had probably played the role of the Queen in *Tasher Desh*. Chhau is a masked dance. Did I get to see any Chhau performances at Santiniketan? I can't remember.

You are not familiar with the name of Haren Ghosh. He was a famous impresario of those times. In other words, he'd use his connections to organize the staging of cultural shows (dance or theatre). In 1940, he brought out a remarkable journal called *Four Arts*. It had a golden cover. It had articles on Uday Shankar, Bala Saraswati, and so many other personages! I have seen the journal *Marg*, which appeared later. It is not like *Four Arts*.

In 1946, a terrible riot broke out in Kolkata. Many innocent people lost their lives. That was when Haren Ghosh was killed.

Amala Shankar and Shanu Lahiri (she was very young then) may know the name of this outstanding Bengali impresario.

We tend to forget things easily. We get too excited about new things, and utterly neglect the old. That is a great pity. Whatever we take pride in, is bound to have a history, after all! Without the past, there can be no present. Without the present, the future cannot take shape. A house without firm foundations is bound to collapse.

Anyway, at the Surul Mela, Haren Ghosh asked me:

'What do you want to eat?'

I pointed at something v-e-r-y expensive and extremely rare: a small tin of condensed milk, priced at four annas. The shopkeeper punctured a hole in it. In supreme bliss, I sucked the sweet, thickened milk from the tin. You have never seen tins of condensed milk. To put it briefly, they contained well-sweetened, densely thickened milk, what we call kheer.

Of course, you haven't seen Nestle's chocolate either. Open the wrapping, and you'd find the picture of a film star of those times. 99 per cent of those film celebrities were from America—famous for their roles in American films. Such as Greta Garbo, Norma Shearer, Charles Laughton, Charlie Chaplin, Ronald Coleman, Bette Davis, and so many others. From the world of Indian cinema, only one person's picture figured in that series. Whether it was Umashashi or Malina Devi, I forget. The image was from the film *Bedouin*.

Nestle's would also offer an album in which those pictures were to be pasted. When the album became full, one would be eligible for a prize. Ritwik's twin sister Pratiti had somehow managed to complete her album. The prize she received was an exquisitely beautiful necklace of false pearls.

In the rainy season, Halakarshan, the ploughing festival, was celebrated in Surul, followed by Briksharopan, the festival of tree plantation. All of us sang together, our voices ringing in the sky: *Maru bijoyer ketan urao.* I remember one such occasion. At Bhubandanga, along the edge of the dam, the ashram dwellers were dancing in a procession. Afterwards, trees were ceremonially planted.

Barshamangal, of course, was an occasion to welcome and celebrate the rains. So many rain songs! So many dances to accompany the songs!

In the month of Bhadra came the Bhadrotsav festival. In the evening, inside the glass temple, the glow of candlelight. I remember the Bhadrotsav songs, *Andhaar elo boley* and *Arup tomar bani.*

In the month of Agrahayan, to celebrate the newly harvested paddy, kheer would be prepared in the kitchen with notun gur, fresh molasses of the season, and notun chal, the fresh crop of rice.

And then came the Poush Mela.

I have already described the contours of the ashram in those days. The venue of the Poush Mela, at that time, stretched from the gate in front of the Mandir, straight up to the Tata building. Stalls were set up on both sides of the street. And the Santhal women would arrive. On either side of the street, they'd spread their wares, selling earrings made of rupadasta.

The word rupadasta figures in the writings of Tarasankar Bandyopadhyay. Even today, rupadasta ornaments are sold at the Poush Mela in Santiniketan. I looked for a female expert on the subject. Well, my younger sister Soma (Ghatak, later

Mukhopadhyay), a regular visitor to the mela, informed me that my sisters, all three of them, had purchased and worn a lot of those ornaments. If kept in a sealed box, the silver sheen retains its brightness, but after a while it turns dull.

The merchandise in the stalls was not very expensive. Squatting on the ground, the sellers would prepare boiled eggs for sale. Frying pantua, they'd steep the sweets in syrup. We also saw a lot of tal-gur patali, blocks of molasses made from toddy-palm juice, similar in appearance to the date-palm patali called khejure gur. The tal-gur patali was locally known as lobat. Never mind if it was not khejure gur. We were always famished, after all. So, we consumed the lobat, flavoured with the chutney of our hunger. Do you understand what the chutney of hunger means? If one is hungry, everything tastes like amrita, the nectar of the gods.

At that mela, the college students of Siksha Bhavana put up a stall with the literary name 'Sahityika', though the wares on sale were tea and vegetable chops. What joy in that enterprise! The girls of Kala Bhavana strung flowerbuds on leaves to create amazing ornaments for sale.

Our gaze, and our hearts, were drawn irresistibly to the fair at the left edge of the field, quite a distance away. It was straight out of *Kumor parar gorur gadi*, the rhyme about bullock carts from the potters' village. There, one found bullock cart wheels, door and window panels, ploughs, yokes, large wooden trays called barkosh, iron ladles, khunti, tongs, karahis, and such other items of merchandise. The buyers and sellers were people from the village, all of them. Santinketan was not as vast then as it is now. The villages were not so remote.

How cold, how bitterly cold it was! The Santhals and other vendors, and the ashram dwellers who had to stay up all night, would all collect twigs and light bonfires.

The mela lasted three days, from the seventh to the ninth of the month. On the ninth of Poush, a display of fireworks would take place. And the Bauls would sing all night long. Did the mela draw even a thousand people, or two thousand? Those days, for all the villagers in the vicinity, it was the fair dearest to their hearts. Musical instruments like bamboo flutes, horn-like bhenpus, earthen tamtemis—it was a mela close to the soil, close to the heart.

On the tenth of Poush, one raced to the site. There before us was the dismantled fairground, enough to make one cry. The mela was over, crowds dispersing, merchandise being packed up, ash from the burnt wood flying in the air.

At my first mela, guess how much I earned? On the first day four annas, on the second, eight annas, on the third, one rupee. That is what I remember. That amount was not to be sneezed at. I could even afford to buy dolls for my siblings, after all. Once, Chhotomama bought me a tiny lantern in the shape of a parrot, made of green glass. It held a light the size of a torchlight bulb. Tucking our earnings into our pockets, we'd clutch at the elbow of any adult in view, student or teacher, and pointing at some food item, plead:

'Can I have that to eat?'

Kinkar-da would feed us anytime we asked. Everyone did.

The day the fair ended, the members of Siksha Bhavana, Kala Bhavana and Sangit Bhavana would set out on a ten-day excursion, singing *Amader Santiniketan*. On one occasion, the infant and middle-school sections of Patha Bhavana struck it lucky. We travelled to Bakreswar. Bathed in the hot spring. What else did we do there?

Actually, those days, Santiniketan kept its youngsters cocooned in a very sheltered, caring atmosphere. When we got back from our trip, drowsy, almost dropping off to sleep, the didis, our caregivers, sponged our limbs, massaged our bodies with warm oil. In the morning, they'd bathe us in water warmed on Jaidev's stove. In the bitter cold, we'd crawl into our quilts and fall asleep.

After winter came the spring. Budding blossoms on the sal trees, palash and shimul in full bloom, and the breeze in that month of Phagun. In the streets, the older boys passed by in procession, singing *Ogo kishor aji*. And all day, one sang *Khol dwar khol, laglo je dol*. All day long, during the spring festival called Basantotsav, we sang and danced, and smeared each other with the colours of abeer. Music and dance performances in the evening. Mohor would burst into song: *Basantey aaj dharar chitta holo utala*.

How our didis struggled that day, scrubbing our heads to remove those colours! Who knew of shampoo then? Our scalps were scoured with heavy detergent soap. When our hair dried, how we craved to run free with those flyaway tresses! But there was no possibility of that. In the evening, the didis would massage the scalp with coconut oil, and insist on securing the hair at the roots before braiding it tightly. Was there any chance, then, of roaming about with a somewhat fancy appearance?

Our mothers didn't even know of the persons who showered such care on their beloved little dolls. Staying in hostel, we still came home without lice in our hair. That was no small matter.

Today it seems to me that every festival in Santiniketan offered homage to the seasons in some form or other. The synchronization of festivals with the seasons has been a continuous tradition in the agricultural life of Adivasis and other farmers. Much later I learnt that the festivals of Santhals and other adivasis are expressions of respect for farming and forest life. They are forms of nature worship based on an awareness of the earth as our primal mother.

In Santiniketan, I have viewed the cycle of seasons in its own glory. Casting one's vision beyond the horizon, without any hindrance. And how exquisite the undulating expanse of the Khowai!

In each separate season, the touch, flow and fragrance of the breeze, also had a distinctive feel. With aroma accompanying the month of Chaitra, the melancholy mood of falling leaves. In winter, the leaves had fallen already, and new leaves had appeared in the month of Phagun. Still, unaccountably, the smell of dead leaves could be felt in the Chaitra winds. The winds of Chaitra and Baisakh set up small whirlwinds of red dust. Every sight you beheld felt extraordinary.

Rabindranath had described the blazing sun of summer afternoons as 'the sunlit night'. That expression is unutterably dear to me. On such afternoons, complete silence prevailed. Only the cry of a kite, and the repeated kup-kup call of some bird, exhausted in the heat of the sun.

The monsoon no longer arrives with the same ceremonial glory as it used to in Santiniketan. Dense dark sky, flying cranes, flashes of lightning. Above the open fields on the way to the station, clouds descending, and then, a tremendous storm, followed by a thundershower. At Baharampur as well, from 1945 onwards, I witnessed similar scenes.

The rains in Santiniketan were even more glorious. In Bahrampur, the rain came down on green fields. But that red soil of Birbhum was parched and hot, the earth mother lying on a bed of fire in an agony of thirst. The leaves on the trees wilted, and by ten in the morning, the sun grew blazing hot. And then came a deep rumbling, followed by an endless succession of dark clouds. We got to witness the monsoon come rushing in. Filling the horizon, torrents of rain, rushing towards us, like an army of soldiers brandishing their spears.

And after that first shower, the fragrance of damp earth, filling the heart with solace.

As soon as the downpour began, a tide of red water descended on the Kopai. And the mastermoshais would rush to the river, drag us into the water and remain with us to ensure that we did not drown. Donning the damp clothes left of the rivershore, letting the garments dry out on our bodies—that was how Santiniketan could mould our physique, to make it as resilient as the earth.

Indeed, those habits, of drenching oneself in the rain, of plunging into the water upon seeing a river—they have persisted to this day. Nowadays one doesn't get to encounter rivers so frequently. It's rivers like the Kopai that I know best.

Do rivers have family traits? Yes, they do. Rivers that descend from the mountains to flow through the plains have a certain character. And rivers that flow over uneven, undulating, rough, stony, gravelly soil have a different behaviour pattern. That is why I once named a piece of writing 'Ganga-Jamuna-Dulang-Chaka'. I went to Purulia in the autumn of my life. The rivers there, such as Kumari-Chaka-Kshintowa-Kansai, are like the Kopai in nature. The last time I plunged about in a river was in Gujarat, in the waters of the Orsang, which also bears a family likeness to the Kopai.

Santiniketan taught us to recognize the unique glory of each separate season. In early autumn, the sky in Santiniketan shone bright blue, the white clouds floating by in the Sharad season's flawless splendour. If you want to gaze at the clouds, observing their variegated forms, sometimes resembling ocean waves, sometimes a fairy palace, or sometimes boats drifting slowly upon blue waters, then it's the Sharad sky that is most suitable. We did gaze at the clouds like that.

And in the cloud-free, rain-washed sky of Sharad, the stars seemed to come down close. Who taught us to recognize the stars I can't remember. We'd point our fingers to identify them: there was Orion, there the Great Bear, and over there, Scorpio.

The late autumn weather of the Hemanta season was chilly, the cold freezing our muscles. And with Basanta, spring arrived in a burst of joy. Amrakunja would be aglow with mango blossom, palash and shimul flowers. So many birds came flocking there—basantabouri, mouchushi, so many others—one lost count of them.

On white paper, any colour you apply will appear vibrant. Around Santiniketan, the colours of the landscape were neutral and melancholy. On that natural background, each season arrived, painted its own colours on the scene, and departed. Till today, I observe and respond to such things. Santiniketan was aware that the inner eye must be opened in infancy itself.

There was a paucity of green. So, our eyes remained thirsty for the sight of green. When we returned after the Puja break, we'd notice that the grass which had sprouted during the rains had now turned a dark shade of green.

Kitu (Krishna) did not speak much.

'Like a green carpet, isn't it?' she once observed.

So it was, indeed.

Today, the world I am speaking of seems like a dream. If a resident student of Patha Bhavana, from my times or after, had been asked to write their memoirs instead of me, and if they had done so, what a productive accomplishment that would have been! I feel that even the administrators in Santiniketan could have taken up such a mission.

I have learnt that Chhotomama, Sankho Chaudhuri, is writing his memoirs. There, a fund of information on many things about many people will become available.

Yesterday I saw the Sharadiya issue of *Desh* for the year 2000. It was a pleasure to see 1938 mentioned in Rabindranath's letters.

These are the days of email and dot-coms. They offer our hands some rest, and save time. But Rabindranath—who watched the sunrise daily, stayed up all afternoon communing with the universe, and devoted all his efforts to the running of Santiniketan—used to answer letters in his own hand, using a pen.

I think of that, and every day I feel amazed.

Fragments of Memory

Sometime between '36 and '38, Cheena Bhavana was built. Those were the times when the construction was under way. They stored water in a tank, to be used for the building work.

One day, Tejes-da took us there.

'Look, look! Look at the tadpoles! There, there, those creatures with tails, swimming about—they're tadpoles. When they become frogs, their tails will fall off.'

'Are frogs of any use?' asked Jolly, her face a picture of innocence.

'In the world of nature, every creature has a role. Frogs live on mosquito eggs and larvae. They provide therapeutic treatment for malaria, do you understand?'

'And then?'

'Snakes will swallow the frogs. And the frogs will try to escape.'

'Snakes are so scary!'

'Why? Why do you say that! Frogs are food for snakes, that's why they consume them. In the world of animals, no creature kills another without reason. But humans will kill anybody.'

Now, with every passing day, I see how humans destroy everything. Through the agency of humans, so many species of trees, vines, shrubs and grasses have vanished from the face of the earth—so many species of forest life! Aquatic creatures and fish, so many species of birds, have become extinct, lost forever. Their numbers are countless, and they will never be seen again.

Rabindranath was born in 1861. In his thirty-ninth year, we entered the twentieth century. At the end of the same century, I write this book. In these hundred and thirty-nine years, a great calamity has befallen the natural world, at every level—in the world, in India, in every region of India. Today, using science and technology, it may be possible to build an edifice three hundred stories high. But the balance of nature cannot be restored.

Santiniketan had taught us to love the spirit of life. For the spirit of life has spread its welcome everywhere.

This train of memory tends to get derailed very easily. I was speaking of Cheena Bhavana. Marshal and Madame Chiang Kai-Shek came to attend the foundation ceremony or inauguration of Cheena Bhavana.

That was also the time when Hindi Bhavana was established.

I wrack my brains to recall what else happened between '36 and '38.

In 1938, something extraordinary took place. Mohor recorded a song when she was a mere girl. When we heard that it would be possible to listen to the recorded song, we rushed to her house.

That was the era of mechanically recorded music, which lasted for a long, long time. A 'record' meant a 'disc' to be played on a machine called the gramophone. Putting the disc in place, one turned a handle to wind up the machine. A pin, fixed on something resembling a phone receiver, was placed on the disc, and it would play. So that was koler gaan, music from a machine. At melas held in small towns and large villages, the vendors of koler gaan would play songs on enormous gramophones with horns mounted on them.

At home as well, there was a gramophone manufactured by HMV, the company called His Master's Voice. Many, many records we had. Savitri Krishnan, Kanak Das—we listened to their renderings of Rabindrasangit in our own home.

What excitement, upon hearing that Mohor had recorded a song on just such a machine! That day, many listeners had assembled in the veranda of their house. We felt entranced even before hearing the music. Bula Mahalanobis (brother of Prashanta Mahalanobis) was present. We waited, gazing at Mohor in admiration. Finally, the song was played. It was not a song composed by Rabindranath. I recall some of the lyrics, and part of the tune. In 1990, I even went and sang part of the song to Mohor. Imagine! Me, singing to Mohor! The opening lines:

> Gaan niye mor khela
> Surer badam diye bhasayi
> Amar gaaner bhela . . .

. . . and so on.

Mohor rose very high in our esteem. As if we had to crane our necks to gaze at her. That day when we heard her recorded performance, we felt was if we were floating on air. In our baitalik that morning, did we sing *E din aji kon ghore go khuley dilo dwar?*

I will talk about music later. All sorts of other memories crowd the mind. This journey down memory lane is extremely whimsical, though. What comes to mind at a particular moment, and where those memories may surface from, no one can predict. I certainly can't.

How old I have grown! Best to acknowledge, at this point, that I have achieved the wisdom of knowing that I know nothing.

Since so much time has gone by in a state of ignorance, what remains of my life will also pass in the same way.

The Things That Come to Mind

Why haven't I told you about our annual games tournament? Yes, I'm referring to what they call 'sports'. It used to happen, indeed, with a lot of joy and merriment.

What events did I take part in? The races! Running with a clay pot on one's head, in what they called a 'balance race'. A spoon in one's mouth, and on it, a potato. You had to hold the spoon handle between your teeth as you ran.

'Ha-du-du' or 'Chu-kit-kit', the race to repeat the sound 'kit-kit' in a single breath for the longest time while trying to touch the opponents so they'd become 'mor' and be forced to sit down.

And then, the skipping race! What excitement, what sheer joy!

The boys' pillow fight was a hilarious competition. A sturdy bamboo pole would be placed horizontally, held aloft by a pair of crossed bamboos at each end. The competitors would sit astride the pole, their legs hugging the bamboo for balance. Then they would attack each other with pillows, hitting away until one of them managed to tip the other off the bamboo. The one who remained atop the pole was the victor. What excitement! Pillows bursting, cotton fluff flying about, the onlookers shouting their encouragement. What a tremendous thrill!

How varied they were, all those games we played!

Hasi-di (Protima Senroy/Roychoudhuri) and Arati-di were daughters of the famous film director Bimal Roy. Later, in my college days, I got to see their younger sister Sonali (Dasgupta/ Rosselini). Hasi-di, a very senior student, was tall, slim and extremely beautiful. She was expert at 'Chu-kit-kit', as she could hold her breath for very long spells. Because of her height, she was also very good at basketball. She'd hum the song *Chaitra pabane mama chitta baney.*

Once we, the little girls, created a low sandcastle in the field in front of Sri Bhavana. That day a tremendous rainstorm broke out, and Shyamoli, being a house made of clay, suffered some damage. Whether the structure broke, or parts of it melted, I can't say. Early next morning, we returned to the spot and found to our amazement that the storm had spared our sandcastle. Sudha-di used to explain everything through rational argument. She reasoned that despite the downpour and the gale, our creation had clearly escaped being hit by a gust of rain.

'Look at that!' we said to each other. 'Shyamoli collapsed, but our house of sand remains intact.'

How little it took to make us happy! Happiness in making a house of sand. Happiness in trying to create a lamp out of clay. Exultation if we managed to steal guavas from the place where Mira-di (Rabindranath's youngest daughter) lived.

I don't thing we received any marks for the schoolwork done in our exercise books. Our work was probably graded: A, B, C. I also remember that there were no annual examinations.

Academic work, discipline, performance in sports, dance, music, in other words, our ability to immerse ourselves in the everyday life of the ashram—probably those were the criteria by which we were assessed, through the year.

Did we even follow the 'Pass' and 'Fail' system? Those of us studying in Class Five were the ones promoted to Class Six. That was the custom. Santiniketan did not adopt any measure that would jeopardize the children's sense of confidence and security. The attempt was to instil in everyone the conviction that if one tried, one could achieve e-v-e-r-y-thing. Can such an instance be found anywhere else?

That was precisely what made Rabindranath's philosophy of child education so unique. He was a creator who moulded human character. He knew that children, when they grow up, will choose their paths according to their individual capacities. But his concern was to ensure that the child learnt to use time productively and find joy in active effort. We were also trained us to think for ourselves and apply our ideas in practice.

The economic backgrounds we came from—who belonged to the middle class, who was the daughter of a land-owning zamindar—such things never occurred to us. Indeed, one encountered some princesses in Patha Bhavana, and later in Siksha Bhavana. Such as the beautiful girls, Ila and Kamal, royals from Cooch Bihar. And Binodini of the Manipur royal family, as well as several others! In college, one met Nikhad Shamsad, daughter of an aristocratic Hyderabad family. (Was she in Sangit Bhavana? or Kala Bhavana? I can't remember.) From Nepal came Swarnakesari and her brother, scions of an elite family. Even in the Santiniketan winter, they found the weather hot, I remember.

During those childhood days in Santiniketan, all of us followed the same discipline. Perhaps for that reason, economic privilege made no dent in one's consciousness. This coincided with the family values one had inherited. Moreover, having come in contact with larger-than-life personages whose greatness of spirit was beyond measure, one no longer feels overwhelmed by people of a lesser stature. Mastermoshai used to go about in short-sleeved phatua and dhoti. Kinkar-da always remained the Kinkar-da we knew, with his long panjabi, short pyjamas, shaggy mop of hair and ever-smiling face and eyes. Chhotey Pandit-ji looked like an ascetic. We never surmised that he'd later gain such fame for his learning.

Did we surmise, for that matter, that Rani Chanda would go on to write such books? Or that a day would come when one could find the students of Mastermoshai and Kinkar-da in all parts of the country? Suren Kar, architect and master builder of the Santiniketan buildings, was a diminutive, polite person.

In dress and deportment, all them looked ordinary in the extreme.

When I returned home, I'd practise the skills I had acquired. I could create exquisite alpana designs. In my own kingdom, I'd bathe my siblings just the way the didis at school used to bathe me. Talk of inculcating a sense of responsibility!

I prompt my pen to write about our literary gatherings. In Patha Bhavana, all three sections held literary meetings. Imagine how we elementary-school students in Class Five and Six organized literary meetings! It was your responsibility, for you to handle!

The Singha Sadana floor was the venue for our gatherings. A low platform served as the stage. How that stage would be decorated, who would preside, how many readings would take place, who would read their own work—you had to decide all these things yourselves. In other words, the entire responsibility was yours. And that was how you absorbed the training in accepting and fulfilling responsibilities. In other words, care was taken to ensure that we developed these capacities.

The best thing was, our assumption of this responsibility also seemed like a natural part of our daily life. And so it happened, in every matter. The natural world follows a regular pattern, taking lessons from nature itself. The rules that govern nature suffer no breaks in their rhythm. Now of course, hunted down by human aggression and greed, even nature has arrived at a critical predicament. With great expectation I wait and watch, for the moment when nature will strike back, like a cornered snake. Not that it doesn't retaliate. In our world, earthquakes, floods and tornados are forms of nature's revenge.

Anyway, let that be. I was speaking of literary gatherings.

To assume the role of editor at a literary meeting was a great honour. And in selecting the readers and their readings, our Bengali teachers also helped us indirectly, from offstage, as it were. What help did they offer? In class, they taught all students to express their thoughts independently in their writing. To what extent the teachers could enthuse us about reading and writing, how much we could absorb—these things too were indirectly tested.

The editor would invite contributions, and we would submit our work. As for rejecting our submissions during the process of selection, such things never happened. Reject our work? The editors had to step out of Singha Sadana, after all. When they emerged, would we have spared them, let them go scot free?

Sulking and muttered complaints were unheard of. All matters were resolved very quickly.

And afterwards, those writings would be read in public. Everyone would listen. 'Sadhu! Sadhu!' they'd always say, by way of applause. But a few opinions would also be expressed. The person who chaired the session would analyse the work at some length. 'Writers' workshop' is a term one has encountered much later. In the 1930s, in India under British rule, such events happened in Rabindranath's Santiniketan.

On one occasion, we enjoyed a great victory in the presidential elections. Sarala Devi Chaudhurani, daughter of Swarnakumari Devi, Rabindranath's younger didi, had come to Santiniketan. Her autobiography *Jibaner Jharapata* is a must-read. The spirited Sarala Devi Chaudhurani, inspired by the ideal of freedom, once organized the Birashtami festival to create a band of people dedicated to the nation's service. And she was the one who first set 'Bande Mataram' to music. From her very photograph we can see what a glowing, confident presence she had. She composed many songs as well.

Bouthan had arrived at Sri Bhavana that evening, accompanied by the famed Sarala Devi. We touched her feet respectfully, and at the same time held out our autograph books. In that autograph book of mine—the one that changed hands even before the dawn of Independence—she inscribed a fragment of song from her own famous composition. I remember the opening lines:

> *Bhedaripunashini! Mama vani!*
> *Gaho aji eikataan!*

The very same Sarala Devi presided over our literary gathering. At that time, I was reading and re-reading *Galpaguchchha*. I had written an analysis of the story 'Chhuti'. That was the piece I read out. Now I realize how stupid I was! Overwhelmed by emotion, I had responded to the story with fulsome praise. And I had also published my views on Rabindranath's *Chhelebela* in the Calcutta paper *Rangmashal*. I was utterly senseless and precocious. With endless patience, Sarala Devi had discussed each piece of writing. How many people can boast of such good fortune!

'Whatever you do, do it on your own'—the value of this training is beyond measure. Do it yourself—or yourselves. From your very childhood, become independent in your thoughts and deeds. But don't break the discipline. Learn to be independent human beings even while observing the rules.

Neither Great nor Small

They were what they were, but they remained an inseparable part of the ashram. The ones I speak of now are profoundly connected with my childhood memories of the ashram. Many can recall the days when we studied in Class Two or Three.

I'm told Dinendranath Tagore once kept a pet deer. That must have been long before our time.

The ones who first come to mind are the swans. Between '36 and '38, I saw several swans in the ashram. Truth be told, swans, peacocks and sundry other birds so highly admired, so eloquently praised in ancient poetry, are terribly nasty species. Bad-tempered they are, and aggressive too. Swans chase after people to bite them.

Peacocks don't fly about much, but they come at you and give you a kick. While working on *Jhansir Rani* (*Queen of Jhansi*), I visited Jhansi and Gwalior in the 1950s. At that time, I noticed that peacocks don't care for humans at all. They are not city creatures, but those days, there were ponds and forests near the city. The peacocks lived in those areas but made forays into the city. In both cities, and in that entire region, there was the widespread practice of making bori, pickles and papad at home. And these would be spread out to dry in the sun. Flocks of peacocks would descend on the stuff and dance on it. If wheat or corn was left out in the sun, they'd gobble it up. If given chase, they'd attack the pursuers, kicking them with their strong, tough legs. All those years ago, there used to be many forests, and many peacocks too.

'What do you do about the menace?' I asked the local people.

'Nothing at all,' they'd reply. 'The peacock is our national bird!'

Peacocks, hens, red junglefowl, they all belong to the same species. Peacocks have great expertise in raiding fields to devour ripe wheat and bajra. Don't imagine that nobody hunts peacocks in secret, to consume their flesh. Those days, people certainly did. But they did it by stealth.

The beauty of swans is beyond compare. The grace with which they swim is glorious, too. But if you approach them, they come squawking at you to give chase. If you insist that swans are non-aggressive, I won't accept that. I have seen them attack people.

Of course, my own encounters with swans took place long ago, in the Santiniketan of those days. Yes, indeed, there were swans in Santiniketan. I don't remember any water body in the ashram though. Nor did I see any swans in the pond on the way to Mamata-di's house. After lunch, it was the responsibility of the senior boys to set forth, carrying brass buckets full of rice and dal to feed the swans. They'd quickly pour out the food at the appointed spot and run away. Because the swans would come rushing at them, flapping their wings and squawking in their harsh voices.

Even Tejes-da failed to find any arguments in support of swans when they were described as irritable and aggressive. Swans have their own unique character. They are unlike any other bird.

'Are swans the same as cuckoos, that they should be expected to sing sweetly?' our mathematics teacher Jaganbandhu-da would demand.

Swans belong to the first category of creatures that I'm speaking of. Next, we need to talk about donkeys.

On Wednesdays, the dhobis would load the laundry on the donkeys' backs and come to the ashram. They'd deliver the laundry to the Dwarik, Vinaya Bhavana and Kala Bhavana hostels, and collect all the soiled clothes. They offered the same service at the teachers' residences at Gurupalli and other buildings. Teachers who had families with them lived in Gurupalli, in mud houses with thatched roofs. Those who lived alone stayed elsewhere.

So, the dhobis spent a great deal of time going about with their donkeys! And after moving around all day, they'd spend the night somewhere in the open, such as the sports ground or the field outside Gour Prangan.

Not for swans or peacocks, but for donkeys, I have long harboured a profound tenderness. Have any of you seen baby donkeys? Covered in long fur, how innocent and beautiful they look! Looking at them, you can't tell that they will grow up to be beasts of burden, symbols of mute labour.

Donkeys were wild creatures once. Else, would wild asses exist even today? It feels good to know that somewhere they still live in the freedom of the jungle.

For three years or so, in Gujarat, I saw only tame donkeys, dark-skinned and very attractive. I have never seen donkeys like that anywhere else. I saw white donkeys there as well, but they were not as good looking as the dark ones.

Lakshman Gaekwad of Muthai once gathered an assembly of ten thousand people and stirred up the town with slogans: 'Give donkeys due respect. Donkeys are the living embodiments of an entire work culture. They labour in silence. They don't shirk.' A single slogan expressed all these sentiments:

Gadha ayaa kursi choro

Let the donkey take the reins, and it will slave for eighteen hours.

Needless to say, no one was pleased with him for uttering such home truths.

Take the donkeys of Santiniketan, for instance. Sleeping in the open fields, chewing on grass if they found some. But upon sighting a full moon in the sky, they'd start braying at the top of their voices. Everyone in the ashram had the right to natural self-expression, after all.

They'd bray, and bray, and bray.

Now for the dogs at Santiniketan. There was no dearth of rustic, uncomplicated, local dogs there, either. They too lived on leftover rice and dal. Basically, a vegetarian diet.

'In summer, dogs go mad, and it's the administration that kills them'. So it was said. But such things never happened in Santiniketan. Once there was a rumour, no doubt. And someone had given that rumour tremendous importance too. What was the outcome? It could not have been pleasant. But after so many years, one doesn't feel inclined to probe such memories.

On moonlit nights, these dogs seemed to undergo a transformation. In a state of immense ecstasy, they'd take to the field, playing, running about. And raising their heads, they would bay at the moon. They lived by their own natural instincts.

With all forms of life in the world of nature—vegetation, living creatures—humans have no natural consonance, I am convinced.

This conviction struck me afresh in September 1998. I was returning from some remote rural area in Maharashtra. All of us were exhausted, and my fellow passengers had fallen asleep. In the west, the sun was sinking. That was western Maharashtra, hence the sun went down very slowly, and even after sunset, it took very, very long for the darkness of night to descend. Apart from the driver and me, nobody else was awake. On both sides, beyond the vast stretches of rough, gravelly, stony terrain, rose waves of low hills at the horizon. Part of the Sahyadri range, maybe. I'm not sure.

Somewhere deep down within me, I had grown calm. The tranquillity of the evening was descending into my inner soul. Long, very long it took, for darkness to descend, drowning the plains and hills. The awareness that awakened within me that evening is something I have treasured in my heart. This is what happened. Suddenly a truth dawned on me. These hills, this plain—how ancient they were, and how worthless was human life in comparison! These hills and fields, all things in the realm of nature, are utterly indifferent to human life. Let all man-made creations be erased, but the sun will still rise and set, just as before.

We have probably covered all there is to say about the Santiniketan of those days. But then, even after narrating everything,

everything can't be said. Some things are lost. Do they really disappear? Like weeds in water, they sometimes float up in our memory, and sometimes vanish into its depths. When they rise to the surface of the mind's lake, one's memory awakens.

I went back to Santiniketan in 1944, as a college student. The donkeys were still there. So were the dogs. But where had all the swans gone?

In the Language of Song

I must say that the number of Tagore songs I can still sing to myself far exceeds what I learnt in my Rabindrasangit class.

In Santiniketan, everyone sang, and many knew how to sing. How did this happen? Well, I've already told you about our work schedule. Work went on, day and night, in the Santiniketan of those times. Santiniketan got us to perform our duties, without ever bullying us, as if to say, 'Get on with it! It's time for class.' What you did, you did of your own accord. Acting on your own sense of responsibility. That was true of music as well.

After all, it wasn't as if class was the only place where you acquired music. In Santiniketan, vast waves of song seemed to constantly heave and swell. Unbeknownst to ourselves, we listened, and absorbed the music. Those destined to become living legends later sang wonderfully, no doubt. But along with them, all of us were also learning and singing an endless stream of songs. There was never a time of day when some song or other was not being sung by some individual or group.

The first time I visited Sangit Bhavana, I remember, was when they were offering a farewell felicitation to Hemendralal

Roy. I dimly recall his bright complexion and his sober, serene appearance.

I have already told you about the Sangit Bhavana of those days. Sangit Bhavana and the Co-Op building were built in the Bengali style, tin-roofed structures designed like mud huts. In Sangit Bhavana, Sailaja-da taught vocal music, accompanying himself on the esraj, in a room at the centre of the building. The small veranda was flanked by a small room on either side. In the room on the right, Ashes Bandyopadhyay gave lessons in Hindi music. From what I recall, he played the esraj. And in his classroom, we sang:

> *Aju Kanha mohe liye*
> *Bansuri bajay ke*

I'm sure I got that wrong. Pushpa Tarawe from Kala Bhavana used to sing a Hindi devotional song addressed to Ganesha, and dance to it.

Sailaja-da was very strict about pronunciation.

'The line is: *Ashaadh, kotha hotey aaj peli chhara*,' he'd say. 'The word is Ashaadh—not Ashaarh.'

Not ashaarh but ashaadh, not amrit but amrut—we learnt these things from Sailaja-da. This training proved valuable during my attempts at recitation (abrutti not abritti), all through my schooldays. Although, on the verge of crossing seventy-five, one must sadly admit that one can't pronounce any words distinctly any more. That is why I have grown so close to the Sabars. They are not particular about pronunciation.

As for Rabindranath's songs, I have been listening to them continuously, since my infancy. Nobody had even thought of sending me to Santiniketan then. Who sends a child to hostel at the age of five? I've been listening to music virtually from the dawning of my consciousness. Baba would buy every record that came out. Amala Das, Kanak Das, Savitri Krishnan, Amita Basu (?)—I listened to their music. In the same measure I also heard Pankaj Mullick and Kanan Devi. It was through my father that I received the maximum exposure to music. When I was five or six, I learnt from him the songs *Door deshi oi rakhal chhele* and *Oder sathey melao*. Sometimes Baba and I would sing together. That too seems like a dream now.

Those days, our lives in the ashram were steeped in song. During the nocturnal procession, when the songs *Je raatey mor* and *Bipul taranga re* made the air reverberate in deep sonorous tones, one felt as if one had floated up to the stars. Baba's elder sister, my pishi Tapati, was a superb singer. His younger sister, my chhotopishi Pratiti, is also an excellent singer, but of late she has decided she can't sing.

Ma's younger sister, my Chhotomashi, Swapnamoyi, was a talented singer, but she began her training with Hindustani dhrupad music. She never got to live in Santiniketan, after all. But Ma's younger brother, my Chhotomama, Sankho, did reside there for many years. He sang a lot, and continues to sing even now, at the age of eighty-five.

But during my time in Santiniketan, how forceful was the torrent of energy that flowed from the source the river of creativity descending from the snow-capped mountain peak! When I consider that even in 1936–38, Rabindranath was still composing dance dramas and creating a steady flow of songs, I realize that the irrepressible force of that torrent of creativity had indeed remained undiminished. I don't know of any other person who remained so alive, creative and indomitable to the very end of his life.

Our day began with song. Rushing outdoors to get drenched in the rain, you sang. You sang at Barshamangal, and at Basanto-tsav. There were no fixed hours for singing. One listened, and one sang.

And between song and season, what extraordinary harmony! Even today, if one hears the songs *Chaitra pabaney* or *Shukno pata ke jhoraye*, it is the warm month of Chaitra in Santiniketan that one remembers. As I have recounted, we felt the change of seasons in our hearts. My memories of music remain intertwined with that experience. Santiniketan taught one to drink in the elements of life and nature with all of one's senses, as if one were dying of thirst. That was the soul of the music.

After leaving Santiniketan, year after year, I have sung song after song for everyone. If you knew how to sing, you sang. Sang spontaneously, from the heart. It was not the ashram that taught us to sing, after all! Listening to the music, we found our voices awakening to song.

At Sangit Bhavana, there was a blind boy named Kalu. When he sang, we used to listen, entranced. Where has that music vanished, now?

Those days, truly talented musicians didn't need books or notebooks when they sang. They had the esraj for accompaniment. And this practice, of singing without the help of written lyrics—it entered one's very bloodstream. I don't know if this is true of most singers of our time, but even an amateur singer like me can still sing from memory, drawing on a repertoire of several hundred songs. When I find listeners, in a different place.

Ours was the era of full-throated song. Singing at the top of our voices, pouring everything we had—our health, our inner energy, our all—into the joy of singing.

After the age of twelve, I no longer lived in Santiniketan. But I had carried the music with me. I used to sing for Ma. And at the ashram, the practice continued, of ceremonially welcoming each new day with song.

Poush Mela 1938

What can one say about the Poush Mela of 1938? It was in December 1938 that I had been taken away from the ashram, after all. A tremendous blow that rendered me mute. An experience that cannot be explained in words. I don't know, in the years that followed, how many others had to leave in a similar fashion, taken away from Santiniketan by their folks at home. I don't know how they had felt.

At that time, for a whole year, what weighed down my heart with grief was the fact that no one had disclosed to me that when I departed, expecting a vacation of ten to fifteen days, I was really leaving the ashram for good. Why did no one tell me that?

I didn't get a chance to say goodbye to anyone. In the new year, when they entered Class Eight, they all got to know: Khuku would not be back.

Why had I left without telling anyone? Just to get an answer to this question, Padma-di, Mira-di and several others—the ones who used to go back and forth between Kolkata and Santiniketan—paid us a surprise visit one day. They turned up at our doorstep.

Ah, what a sight that was! Back in Kolkata, I had to take to wearing saris. Sari to school, sari at home. Facing those visitors, I remember how confused I felt about myself.

So, that's the Poush Mela we are speaking of. All of us woke up very early. It was the sixth of Poush, the regular date for the mela. Stalls being set up. Hearts full of joy. After the mela ended, the students of Siksha Bhavana, Kala Bhavana and Sangit Bhavana, along with their teachers, would go off on separate excursions. Later, we too as Siksha Bhavana students had gone to Dumka, Ghatshila, Jamshedpur.

Our minds were dazzled by the joy of Poush Mela. What magic in that festival! Even bathing at the crack of dawn didn't seem so difficult. Then, on to the kitchen to devour luchi, bondey, pantua.

Off to the Mandir after that. The Mandir, teeming with people that morning. I remember Hasi-di on the Mandir steps with Anita-di beside her, beautiful in their white silk saris and Santhal earrings. Their presence lit up the stairs. With them I think was Maitreyi Devi, who was usually present on that occasion.

See, now, I am reminded of some people about whom I haven't spoken. Deepti and Tripti, Banaphool's sisters-in-law, were there. Their brothers were members of the ashram too.

The alpana designs on the Mandir floor were created by the Kala Bhavana girls, under the supervision of Gouri-di (Gouri Bhanja).

We little ones sat there waiting, dressed in warm clothes and our best outfits. What were our warm clothes and best outfits like? We must not forget that the offspring of Didima, my maternal grandmother, were devout swadeshis. My mother, who believed in fabric that was coarse and dull, never knitted any woollen garments. Later, Bhalomashi (Shakuntala) and Chhoto-mashi knitted sweaters for us.

We went to the festival wearing what clothes we had. Having combed our heavily oiled hair and bathed after soaking ourselves in mustard oil, we little ones took our places there with hearts full of joy. Luckily for us, nobody said:

'Ai! Why are you dressed like that?'

Today, the celebrations at the Mandir on the seventh of Poush remain the same as in our times. The practices of those days must surely have continued unchanged, to this day. All the festivals I've described are still observed, that's for sure.

So, we have come to the end. The end of all that I witnessed while Rabindranath was alive. That is what I narrate here, from memory.

First, the chanting of Vedic songs. Then, in consonance with what Rabindranath spoke of in his lecture, the performance of songs from the 'Puja' section of his compositions. I had a conversation with Jayashri (Chanda/Sen). They had heard Kshitimo-han Sen reciting the prayers at the festival. We too had heard him, in Patha Bhavana and Siksha Bhavana. Visva-Bharati had not yet become a Central University, at that time.

So, at the festival on the seventh of Poush, all of us celebrated in joy. No shadow of the future had marred our bliss. I did not know that three days later, on the tenth of Poush, I would be leaving for home, but not on vacation. I would be leaving Santi-niketan for good. Chhotomashi knew all about it, but she did not tell me anything.

It took me a long time to forget the rage and bitterness I would harbour against Chhotomashi. She was merely following instructions. But I was not mature enough to understand that then.

Six months later, I expressed my rage. Between June and July 1939, three family weddings took place. The weddings of Mejomama (Debu Chaudhuri), Sejokaka (Sudhish Ghatak) and Chhotomashi. Chhotomashi's wedding ceremony took place in Dhaka. In a fit of obstinacy, I refused to go. I had not forgotten my grief at being taken away from Santiniketan.

But during the three days of the Poush Mela, there was only endless bliss.

On the tenth of Poush, Chhotomashi said:

'Come, I'll take you to Kolkata.'

We boarded the train. Merely going on holiday, why would one carry one's bedding? Friends, companions, belongings—so much was left behind. I came away.

After my return to Kolkata, at that tender age of thirteen, I had to absorb the reality that things there could not go on without me. Ma was terribly ill, and bedridden. I was thirteen. We were six siblings then. The youngest, Phalgu, was a little over a year old.

I wept. For many days, I wept. Kolkata Beltola School, home, none of these felt like my own place. Everything struck me as artificial.

From that very day, I had to understand that I was the eldest. All the responsibility was mine. It was as if I had been uprooted from the open sky and outspread fields and locked inside a cage. That grief pierced my heart and lodged there for a very long time. I did not share it with anyone.

For me, 'our Santiniketan' was the place after my own heart. There must surely exist many others like me, each with a special, beloved place of their own. I always feel that a person should not be uprooted in their infancy from their beloved place, in that manner. If you intend to uproot them, you should inform them first.

Children can accept the inevitable. At least in our times, they could. Else, how did I take charge of my younger siblings and become their protector, caring for them without consulting my mother on anything?

Seventh of Poush 1938, you are a day I can never forget.

What I Received, What I Understood

The ideals of education promoted by the Patha Bhavana of those days continued to be practised, long after, by certain schools who managed to follow those ideals to a great extent, even within the constraints of official rules and regulations. The very knowledge of this fact gives one great satisfaction.

From 1944 to 1946, I studied in Santiniketan, after all. It had not changed much, even at that time. And now I hear that Patha Bhavana is a very, very good institution, even today.

It's best to acknowledge that I don't travel to Santiniketan often. I did visit a few years ago. There I learnt that 'our Santiniketan' still remains the same.

Where can it be found? The house named Udayan still exists. But standing in the veranda, I wondered: was this that same spot where *Chitrangada* was performed? I gazed at the staircase leading up to the first floor. This house, that had seemed so enormous once, how tiny it appeared now! A house that seems gigantic in childhood appears small to the adult eye. I have noticed this so often!

But where had the kitchen vanished? Where were all the familiar things of those earlier days? Had I resided in Santiniketan, or visited frequently, I would not have felt so affected by the changes.

Anyway, Santiniketan has grown up. That is inevitable, with the passage of time. Visva-Bharati has become a Central university. So many of Rabindranath's letters express his anxiety about the financial viability of Santiniketan! Today, Visva-Bharati must be free of such worries.

But it's best to articulate what I have felt for many years. The day after tomorrow, I will turn seventy-five. Should I speak now, or later? How much longer will I live, anyway?

Visva-Bharati is a Central university, one of a few such universities in India. I feel that Visva-Bharati could have been developed into a university with a different character. A place where translation and dissemination of literature—the literatures of all the Indian languages into other languages of the world, and translation of world literatures into Indian languages—would be practised. Where students, scholars, researchers, from India and abroad, would come and reside. Research would flourish, and so would publication. The institution could have drawn East and West closer to each other. In the sky of knowledge, there are no borders after all.

In such a place, in the truest sense, the world would reside in one nest.

Patha Bhavana, Kala Bhavana, Sangit Bhavana—these would remain part of the structure, for sure. Alongside, there would be an active exchange of languages, literatures, cultures. That Visva-Bharati, the place I envisaged in my dreams, would have gained tremendous eminence and honour in these last fifty years.

I dream of such a university, created with Rabindranath's name as its central inspiration. That dream is not destined to come true.

If such a university had indeed come into existence, it would not have been extensive in size. Yet it would attract only the truly dedicated and inspired. The significance of the name 'Visva-Bharati' would also expand, crossing all frontiers.

Let me speak in a selfish vein. In those three years there, I received a great deal. It was the mission of the Santiniketan of those days, to open a thousand eyes and doors in the mind, right from one's infancy.

The place imparted to us the lesson that, just as in the realm of nature there is no repose or idleness, so our must our own endeavours ever continue. In the heart of our labour, the stream of bliss would flow. We took that lesson to heart. A great deal we learnt, indeed.

In work resides freedom. In diligence lies bliss. These lessons, too, one learnt in infancy. Let your work be inspired by your own commitment. Your own sense of responsibility.

When I think of that period, it seems that the Patha Bhavana of those days did not harbour the expectation that the youngsters there would grow up to become shining stars. The place had wanted to mould human beings to be diligent, responsible, empathetic and capable of independent thought and active endeavour.

I don't think I have succeeded in meeting those ideals. If I have achieved even a fraction of those visionary goals, it is because of the education I received as a child. As for the rest, the failure is mine.

I have tried to share my memories. Have I succeeded in communicating to you what our Santiniketan was like? What in those days used to be our very own place, the very place where our hearts belonged—that very same Santiniketan!

Personalities (in their order of appearance)

(*With her failing memory at the time of writing, it is possible that Mahasweta Devi mis-remembered some names, or was referring to people whose names are hard to trace in the present day.*)

Ramananda Chattopadhyay (1865–1943): Founder, editor and owner of Calcutta-based magazine, the *Modern Review*. Often described as the 'father of Indian journalism'.

Sankho Chaudhuri (1916–2006): Considered one of the stalwarts of modern Indian sculpture. A student of Ramkinkar Baij, he was best known for his simple, flowing sculptures and his constant experiments with material: clay, terracotta, plaster and cement, stone, wood, copper, brass and aluminium.

Amiya Chakravarty (1901–86): Tagore's secretary, from 1924 to 1933. Also a poet, Chakravarty joined Visva-Bharati in 1921, first as a student and then as a teacher. Accompanied Rabindranath on his tours of Europe and America in 1930 and Iran and Iraq in 1932.

Rathi-da (RathindranathTagore) (1888–1961): Rabindranath's eldest son, and among the earliest graduates of Santiniketan. Studied Agricultural Science at the University of Illinois, and later was the first vice-chancellor of Visva-Bharati. An artist in his own right, he has left behind some beautiful landscapes and paintings of flowers and fauna in the Orientalist style.

Buri-di (Nandita): Daughter of Mira Devi, youngest daughter of Rabindranath Tagore.

Krishna Kripalani (1907–92): Taught at Santiniketan, after enduring imprisonment for his role in the Indian freedom movement. From 1933, until Rabindranath's death in 1941, worked in close association with the poet and edited the *Visva-Bharati Quarterly*, founded and first edited by the poet himself.

Mastermoshai (Nandalal Bose) (1882–1966): One of India's most significant artists of the twentieth century and among the few who sought to reinvigorate Indian art by rooting it in Indian tradition, shunning the overarching Western academic approach that prevailed at the time. A student of Abanindranath, in 1920, he joined Kala Bhavana as a teacher, and in 1922 became its principal. Among his most well-known works are the Haripura paintings, a series of over 80 panels executed on hand-made paper in 1937, painted at Mahatma Gandhi's request to mark the session of the Indian National Congress in Haripura, Gujarat (February 1938).

Tanay-da (Tanayendranath Ghosh) (1895–1958): One of the teachers at Patha Bhavana. Compiled—and published at his own expense—the first *Amader Lekha*, the Patha Bhavana yearbook presenting texts and artworks by the students.

Gaganendranath Tagore (1867–1938): A self-taught artist, and one of the first modern painters of India. Known for his 3 portfolios of cartoons, *Birupa Bajra*, a merciless satire of contemporary Bengal society; the witty caricatures of *Adbhut Lok*, published as *Realm of the Absurd*; and *Naba Hullod* (Reform Screams). Brother of Abanindranath, and nephew of Rabindranath.

Kinkar-da (Ramkinkar Baij) (1906–80): First Indian sculptor to move away from colonial academic practices and give an individualist and modernist turn to Indian sculpture. Best known for his monumental sculptures in Santiniketan. Also an accomplished painter.

Tejeschandra Sen (1893–1960): Teacher of Bengali, English, geography, history, mathematics and nature study along with music and gardening. He was known for his love for nature and is memorialized by Benodebehari in his painting *The Tree Lover*.

Bouthan: Pratima Devi (1893–1969). Daughter of Binayini Devi, sister of Gaganendranath and Abanindranath Tagore. Accompanied Rabindranath and her husband on several of the poet's foreign visits. Brought back the knowledge of many new crafts and incorporated them into the curriculum at Silpa Sadana. Played a significant role in the production of Rabindranath's dance dramas, especially the design of sets and costumes.

Jadupati-da: Possibly Jadupati Basu, student of Nandalal Bose.

Jiban-da: Possibly Dr Jitendranath Chakravarti, medical officer at San-tiniketan.

Hazariprasad Dwivedi (1907–79): Taught Sanskrit and Hindi. Worked in Santiniketan for two decades. Helped found the Hindi Bhavana and was its head for many years. Also founded and edited the *Visva-Bharati Patrika* in Hindi.

Kshitish Roy-da (1911–55): Joined Visva-Bharati as a teacher of English at Siksha Bhavana, in 1934. Was editorial assistant to Krishna Kripalani on the *Visva-Bharati Quarterly*. Was chosen by Tagore to develop and extend the *Sahaj Paths*. After the death of the poet, was Curator of Rabindra Bhavana (1955–61) and worked in close association with Vice-Chancellor Satyendranath Bose on preparing a draft scheme for the reorganization of the Tagore Museum and Archives that could be realized in the Centenary year.

Sishir Mitra-da (1987–1963): Taught at Santiniketan for eight years; left in 1940 to become Professor of Philosophy at Benaras Hindu University.

Haricharan Bandyopadhyay (1867–1959): Rabindranath had written a first book of reading in Sanskrit for his children—Haricharan completed the series, *Sanskrita Prabes,* in three parts. In 1905, Rabindranath asked him to compile a Bengali dictionary—later, published as the 5-volume *Bangiya Sabdakosh* (Bengali dictionary), for which he is remembered even today.

Prabhatkumar Mukhopadhyay (1892–1985): Joined Patha-Bhavana as a librarian and teacher. In 1929, the Rabindra Parichay Sabha, of which he was a founder member, assigned him the task of writing a biography of the poet. The 4-volume work, *Rabindra Jibani* took over 25 years to complete and laid the foundation for further research on Rabindranath.

Kshitimohan Sen (1880–1960): Was principal of Vidya Bhavana, and one of the vice-chancellors of Visva-Bharati. Was awarded the first Desikottama in 1952. Also the grandfather of Nobel Laureate Amartya Sen.

Satyacharan Mukhopadhyay: A doctor by profession and father of Balaichand Mukhopadhyay, also a doctor and better known by his pen name Banaphool.

Upendramohan Das: Possibly Upendra Kumar Das? Teacher of Bengali and later a professor of Bengali.

Anil Kumar Chanda (1906–76): Trained at the London School of Economics. Was secretary to Tagore and principal of the Siksha Bhavana. Later served as a deputy minister in the Government of India.

Sailaja-da (Sailajaranjan Majumdar) (1901–76): Arrived at Visva-Bharati in 1932 as a lecturer in Chemistry, then had an opportunity to learn Rabindranath's songs from the Poet himself as well as from Dinendranath Tagore. Rabindranath was so impressed with his talent in music that, when Sangit Bhavana was established in 1939, he asked Sailajaranjan to take charge of it as the first Principal. He prepared the notations for a vast number of Tagore's songs, published in *Svarabitan* and was a vital part of the plays and dance-dramas produced at that time.

Gosain-ji (Nityanandabinod Goswami) (1907–72): Came to Santiniketan in 1920 as a Research Scholar. Was encouraged by Rabindranath to visit Ceylon and make a special study of the *Abhidhammapitaka*. On his return, he was expected to devote himself to research in Buddhist studies but Rabindranath asked him to teach Bengali and Sanskrit and that is what he did till the end of his service.

Santi-da (Santidev Ghosh) (1910–99): Student at Santiniketan Vidyalaya and later teacher of dance at Patha Bhavana. Principal of Sangit Bhavana (1964–68, 1971–73). Tagore also encouraged Ghosh to act and dance in the dance dramas, for which Ghosh displayed an uncommon talent. In 2002, India released a postage stamp on Ghosh to commemorate his contribution to music.

Jagadananda Roy (1869–1933): First principal of the Brahmacharyasrama. Taught science and mathematics till his retirement in 1932, after which he taught mathematics voluntarily. Wrote a number of books on popular science, including one of the earliest science-fiction stories in Bengali, *Shukra Bhraman* (*Travels to Venus*) in 1892, later published in his book *Prakritiki* (1914).

Mrinalini Swaminathan (later Sarabhai) (1918–2016): Daughter of freedom fighter and later parliamentarian Ammu Swaminathan, she studied dance at Santiniketan. Went on to become a well-known classical dancer, choreographer and fonder director of Darpana Academy of Performing Arts. Was also engaged in the promotion of Indian handicrafts and handloom.

Gurdial Malik (1896–1970): Came to Santiniketan to meet Rabindranath where he also met C. F. Andrews. Taught English literature. In 1928, Rabindranath asked him to teach at Siksha Bhavana. He taught at both school and college, and was the editor of the *Visva-Bharati Quarterly* for a couple of years.

'Andrews-saheb: Charles Freer Andrews (1871–1940), English missionary whose experiences in India led him to advocate for Indian independence and for the rights of Indian labourers around the world. Tagore's calls for social justice and his ideas about the synthesis of Eastern and Western culture strongly shaped Andrews' spiritual and political views, and he chose to spend the rest of his life teaching and working at Santiniketan. 'Dinabandhu' literally translates to 'friend of the poor'.

Binod-da (Binode Bihari Mukhopadhyay) (1904–80): A student of Nandalal Bose, and friend and close associate of Ramkinkar Baij. Inspired many brilliant students over the years, notable among them painter Jahar Dasgupta, Ramananda Bandyopadhyay, K. G. Subramanyan; sculptor and printmaker Somnath Hore; designer Riten Majumdar; and filmmaker Satyajit Ray. In 1949, he left to join as curator the Nepal Government Museum, Kathmandu. In 1958, he returned to Kala Bhavan, and later became its principal.

Amita-di (Amita Sen) (1913–2005): Known as 'Ashram Kanya' or 'daughter of the ashram', she wrote several books on Rabindranath Tagore and Santiniketan. Her father was Kshitimohan Sen and her son is Amartya Sen.

Mohor, and Suchitra: Renowned Rabindrasangit artistes, Kanika Bandyopadhyay (1924–2000, student, and later teacher, Head of the Department of Rabindra Sangit and Principal at Sangit Bhavana); and Suchitra Mitra (1924–2011).

Kalimohan Ghosh (1884–1940): Arrived at Santiniketan in 1907 to assist Rabindranath in his educational mission, especially his village-upliftment efforts. Was sent to England by Rabindranath to study methods used in primary education and adult literacy. Also joined as an able assistant to Leonard Elmhirst when the latter founded the Institute of Rural Reconstruction at Sriniketan.

Haren Ghosh (1895–1947): A successful impresario who promoted Indian music and dance internationally, including Uday Shankar's. He was murdered during the Calcutta riots.

Ashes Bandyopadhyay (Asheschandra Bandyopadhyay) (1920–92): One of the foremost exponents of the esraj in India. Apart from Hindusthani vocal music, he taught Bengali tappa, sitar and the esraj for almost 50 years at Sangit Bhavana.

Maitreyi Devi (1914–89): Poet and novelist, best known for her Sahitya Akademi Award-winning novel, *Na Hanyate* (It Does Not Die).

Gouri-di (Gouri Bhanja) (1907–98): Daughter of Nandalal Bose. Also taught at Kala Bhavana for a few years.

Places

Mandir: Also known as the Upasana Griha, or the Brohmo Mandir, a prayer hall built by Rabindranath'sfather, Debendranath Tagore, on 21 December 1891. Made out of beautiful panels of Belgian stained-glass, it is also often referred to as the 'Kaanchermandir' or 'the glass temple'.

Uttarayan: A complex of five architecturally varied houses named Udayan, Konarka, Shymali, Punascha and Udichi. Except Udayan, the other four are small in scale and Tagore lived in all of them at some point of time.

Kala Bhavana: The art college at Santiniketan founded by Rabindranath in 1919 and headed by Nandalal Bose until 1951. It played an important role in breaking down the conventional division between art and craft, in promoting multi-professionalism and giving a new direction to modern Indian art and art education.

Vinaya Bhavana: The Teachers Training College at Visva Bharati. It began as a training center for teachers in art, craft and music in 1948 and turned into a full-fledged teachers' training college in 1951.

Gourprangan courtyard: The open ground in front of the school building, named after Gour Gopal Ghosh, a student and teacher at Santiniketan

Khowai: a natural canyon formed by the erosion of red laterite soil by water and wind. Only certain types of plants, such as sonajhuri or acacia, can grow there. The Khowai in Santiniketan figures prominently in Tagore's writings.

Flora and Fauna

akanda: Sun-plant, swallow wort

akashnim: Variety of margosa

amlaki: Myrobalan, a small sour fruit

amrul: Indian sorrel, *oxalis corniculata*

anantamul: Medicinal herb

aparajita: Flowering vine

arjun tree: Deciduous tree with medicinal properties

ashok: Tree with deep red flower

ashsheora: Rum berry, *glycosmis pentaphylla*

ata: Custard apple

atasi: Linseed, flax, rattle wort

baheda: Medicinal fruit, *balearica myrobalan*

bakul: Large evergreen tree with white scented flower,

bel: Wood apple

bel pana: Wood-apple beverage

borboti: Kind of kidney bean; *dolichos catjong*

chaalta: Tree with acid fruit

chhatim: Tree with finger-like branches and seven-leaf clusters

dhatura: Thorn apple

gaab: Tree bearing fruit with thick skin, its juice used as coating matter

gokhro: Cobra

gulancha: Heart-leaved moonseed

hasnuhana: Fragrant white flower that blooms in the evening

hele: Halhaliya, a kind of non-venomous snake

jamrul: Small, greenish-white juicy fruit

kadam: Flower; *neolamarckia cadamba*

kalke: Shrub with yellow blossoms

karabi: Oleander

kul: Jujube

madhabilata: *Gaertnera racemose*, a fragrant vine

mahua: Flowering tree, *bassia latifolia*

malati: Variety of jasmine, *jasminum grandiflorum*

palash: Tree with red flowers, *frondosa*

sal: *Vatica robusta*, tree known for its timber

sapeda: Fruit of the sapota

shami tree: Sami or khejri, known for medicinal properties and spiritual associations. Also used as another name for the babla or thorny babul tree from which gum is obtained.

shiuli: White fragrant autumnal flower, *vitex negundo*

sirish: Rain-tree

tal: Palmyra

thankuni: Indian pennywort

Food

bondey: Small globular sweet made of powdered chick-pea dipped in syrup

chire: Flattened rice

habishyanna: Rice cooked in ghee for prayer offerings

luchi: Deep-fried flatbread, made out of white wheat flour

mohonbhog: Semolina pudding

muri: Puffed rice

pantuas: Syrupy sweets

pithe: Can be sweet or savoury, and usually made from a rice-flour dough or batter, which is then steamed, fried or griddled.

Family

dadu: maternal grandfather

didima: maternal grandmother

jyatha: father's elder brother

kaka: father's younger brother

mama: mother's brother

mashi: maternal aunt

pishi: father's sister

thakurda: paternal grandfather

thakuma: paternal grandmother

Some Other Points of Interest

'the primers *Barnaparichay* and *Sahaj Path*': The former ('Introduction to the Alphabets') is by nineteenth-century social reformer and scholar, Ishwarchandra Vidyasagar, and the latter ('Easy Reading') by Rabindranath Tagore, published in 1930 with illustrations by Nandalal Bose.

Poush Mela: An annual fair held at Santiniketan since 1894. It commences on 7 Poush (around 21 December) in remembrance of the initiation of Debendranath into the Brahmo creed on 7 Poush 1843.

Manasamangal: Or, *Manasamangalkavya*. Bengali Hindu religious text, composed more or less between the thirteenth and eighteenth centuries, dedicated to the indigenous deity Manasa, goddess of snakes. Mangal means 'benevolent/benediction', and 'kavya' means poem.

'Ishermul was among the anti-snake trees planted on Santali mountain by Chand Sadagar': Also known as the Ishwarmul tree, or Indian birthwort, used to treat snake bites, diarrhoea, skin and heart diseases, asthma (*Aristolochiaindica* L.). Chand Sadagar was a rich and powerful river and sea merchant and a devote of Siva, who refused to pay obeisance to Manasa.

'Inscribed on it was a Sanskrit phrase': *Yatra visvam bhavatieka nidam* (where the world resides in one nest), the motto selected by Rabindranath for Visva-Bharati.

'I remember very clearly Rabindranath's lecture at the Mandir during my college days': Mahasweta couldn't have heard Rabindranath's lecture during her college days, because he was no longer alive at that time! Earlier she writes that she returned to Santiniketan as a college student in1944. But Rabindranth died in 1941. This is an example of how her memory had started playing tricks and was no longer reliable when she wrote this memoir. One of the instances that corroborates what I say in the Introduction about the unreliable narrator of this text.

'The epic about ants called *Lal–Kalo*': *Lal–Kalo* (Red–Black) is a delightful tale, written for children by Girindrasekhar Bose, chronicling an epic battle between the red ants and the black ants, and the role played by various other animals in it.

'Chhotomama, Sankho Chaudhuri, is writing his memoirs': Sankho Chaudhuri, *SmritiBismriti* (Subarnarekha, 2002).

'Mohor recorded a song when she was a mere girl': Hindustan Records, February 1938. Catalogued as H584, Adhunik.

'In our baitalik that morning, did we sing *Edin aji kon ghore go khuley dilo dwar*?': On the reverse of Mohor's first gramophone record was the song '*Ore oi bandho holo dwar*'. Lyrics: Niharbindu Sen. Music: Haripada Chattopadhyay.

bhenpu: Wind-instrument, producing a hooting sound

bhutni: A female spirit. Later, also petni.

durmush: Rammer

gamchha: Hand-woven towel

garad silk: Undyed silk fabric woven in Murshidabad

ha-du-du: The game of kabaddi

hemanta: Late autumn in the cycle of Bengali seasons

mehendi: Henna

phatua: Short-sleeved upper garment for men

Poush Sankranti: Auspicious day in mid-January when farmers start harvesting crops and prayers are offered for a bumper crop

prabhati: Morning song

shataranchi: Hand-woven chequered rug